Dr. Kalaignar Thiru M. Karunanidhi Endowment Lectures,
Madras University, Madras, 7th, 10th, 11th April, 1995

Landed Elites in Upheaval—Forms and Contents of Resistance by the Palegars—1800-1846

Dr. Kalaignar Thiru M. Karunanidhi Endowment Lectures,

Madras University, Madras, 7th, 10th, 11th April, 1995

Landed Elites in Upheaval—Forms and Contents of Resistance by the Palegars—1800-1846

Dr. J.C. Dua

Originals

Delhi-110052

Published by
Originals
A-6, Nimri Commercial Centre,
Near Ashok Vihar Phase-IV, Delhi-110052
Phones: 27302453
e-mail: lpp@nde.vsnl.net.in
visit us at: www.lppindia.com

First Published 2006

ISBN 81-88629-61-8

Printed at
D K Fine Art Press P. Ltd.
Delhi-110052

PRINTED IN INDIA

Preface

The East India Company had a very active imperialistic interests in India as its very survival as a commercial corporation depended on the preservation of the Indian empire. The history of India, particularly of the last quarter of the eighteenth and first half of the nineteenth centuries, shows that though the meaning of imperialism depended on the goals, intellect, and intensity of interest among individuals and groups involved in India, they had a unanimity on their elemental conviction that British power must be maintained in India.

The palegar resistance could be easily be bracketed together with the spontaneous resistance against the English East India Company which continued in India for nearly hundred years preceding the revolt of 1857. The chief aim of the palegars as was the case with the zamindars of different categories in other parts of India, was to seek greater share in the power over, and thus in the revenues of, their region. They relied mainly on the support from peasants, smaller zamindars/palegsrs and local officials, but that support was forthcoming again because of fear or for promoting individual interests. In the conditions of unfettered political and military adventurism, it is noteworthy that none of the adventurer zamindars/palegars was either strong enough to be able to win allegiance of others or in a position to replace the state power.

As far as the first phase of the palegar resistance during the early 19th century in the Ceded Districts is concerned, it may be observed that if an attempt is made to draw parallels with other such incidents the question of non-acknowledgement of English suzerainty on the part of the palegars may appear as one of the important factors of their resistance. The British occupation was looked upon as nothing short of usurpation of the authority by them. However, this phase of palegar resistance was based on the traditional links and qualified loyalties between the peasants and the palegars. The resistance was wholly local and isolated in character lacking required mass appeal.

While discussing about the nature of the second phase of the palegar resistance, the attempt has been to highlight the comparative change in the political scenario between 1800 and 1845-46. With the lapse of more than four decades the English had acquired vast administrative experience, political authority and military power. They would not hesitate in deviating from the position and policy adopted by the early English administrators in a big way and started completely neglecting the value of the indigenous social and economic traditions and institutions as a means of giving social happiness and material well-being to the people. As such, this phase of resistance was not aimed to gain any political power, as was the case with the palegar resistance of late 18th and early 19th centuries, but was essentially a socio-economic one in which a considerable section of the people felt, however dimly, the stirring of a common impulse.

Though these lectures were delivered way back in April 1995, all along I have been waiting for the Madras University to take the initiative in publishing these lectures. It is primarily due the insistence of and interest shown by some of my fellow colleagues and friends, that I made up my mind to get these lectures published on my own and share my views with other scholars and students interested in the subject.

I am extremely grateful to Professor R. Balasubramanian, Professor Perumal and other members of the Department of Politics and Public Administration, Madras University, Chennai for inviting me to deliver the prestigious Dr. Kalaignar Thiru M. Karunanidhi Endowment Lectures and giving me an opportunity to share my views with other learned scholars of the University. I am also grateful to late Dr. S.P. Gupta, former Secretary, University Grants Commission, New Delhi for persuading me to accept this offer.

No less important has been the support from Principal Deepak Malhotra, Professor Dilbhag Singh (JNU), Lala Bhagwan Dass Goel, former Director Prosecution, Mr. Mohinder Singh, Advocate, Supreme Court, and Mr. Ashok Kumar Singh, Reader in History, Dyal Singh Evening College (University of Delhi) who had been eagerly waiting for this volume.

I would like to express my gratitude towards Mrs. Anita Dua, Silky and above all dear Jimmy.

J.C. Dua

27.3.06

Contents

Glossary of the Words Used

The glossary has been prepared with the help of the books/ source material like, Henry Yule and A.C. Burnell, *Hobson Jobson*; H.H. Wilson, *A Glossary of Judicial and Revenue Terms; Fifth Report*; *The Inam Settlement Papers*; and BK Baden-Powell, *The Land Systems of British India.* However, for certain specific terms, original source material and research articles etc. have also been used. Definitions and derivations, where known, have also been mentioned.

Abbreviations :

(A)	from Arabic
(P)	from Persian
(K)	from Cannada
(S)	from Sanskrit
(T)	from Tamil

Adalat	-	Court of law.
Agraharam	-	A village, or a part of one, occupied by rahmans and held either rent - free or at a favourable rate of assessment.
Amaram	-	Land or revenue granted by a chief to his etainers for military service (Tamil Lexicon, I, p.102). Landgranted n condition of service (could be even for revenue collection), resumable if stipulated service was not performed.
Amil	-	Revenue Collector, Agent, Officer, superintendent of a district or division of a country or pargana. (Almost same as amildar).

Amildar (P) - A Collector of or contractor for revenue, of uniting civil, military and financial powers (a pre-1800 usage in south India).

Asofa,

Asoph (A) - A title given by Tipu Sultan to certain civil officers.

Bakshi,

Bakshshi (P) - A military officer-in-charge for payments of salaries or an officer who kept an account of all disbursements connected with military tenures.

Bhatta,

Batta - Allowance to troops in the field.

Bhatta-vritti - A general term to denote in 'am granted to Brahmans/Hindus for charitable purposes. Secular in 'ams.

Brahmandaya,

Brahmadaya - A general term denoting in 'ams held by Brahmans for their personal benefit.

Chattram - In 'am for the support of a 'Chattram; or halting place for the accommodation of travellers.

Chauth - In theory on-fourth, share of the revenue granted to or exacted by the Marathas, in practice could be more or less than one-fourth.

Chavadi - Same as 'Chattram'.

Choultry - Same as 'Chattram'.

Chowkie, Chowky,

Chokie, Chauki - A place where an officer is stationed to receive tolls and customs.

Cowle, Kaul (A)- Promise, agreement, contract, engagement. An agreement, engagement, or lease of land for the cultivation of land. Generally to large farmers and on favourable terms.

Croe - Equal to .25 to .75 acre.

Daffedar, Dafadar, Duffedar (P) - The commander of a party of a horse and foot soldiers.

Daksinasimp-asandhipati - Viceroy of South.

Dalvai, Dalavay (Tamil :Talavay) (K) - The commander-in-chief, hence also the prune minister under Vijayanagar and Mysore rulers.

Darbar (P)

Darbar- - The court of a king or chief.

Khirch (P) - Court charges.

Dasbhandam - An allowance of land (Khanda Dasbhandam) or of revenue (Shamilat Dasbandham) given as a compensation for the construction of a tank, well, or channel. The grant generally, though not invariably, carried with it the condition of keeping the work in repair.

Desai - Essentially an assessment officer, responsible for the proper assessment and fixation of 'jama' of the cultivated areas of the villages under him; was next to the shiqdar but higher than the other revenue officials like muqaddams, chaudhris and the qanungo who worked under him.

Desmukh - (from S. desa a district, and S. mukha mouth, face front). Headman or Collector of a district or portion of a country; an officer corresponding with zamindar, but more ancient.

Devadayam - Lit. 'Gift to God' in 'ams granted to or for the support of temples. Religious grants; had several sub categories.

Dharmadayam - A general term used to denote in 'am granted for charitable purposes. Secular in 'ams.

Diwan, Dwan (P)- Native minister of the revenue department, and judge in civil causes within his jurisdiction; receiver-general of a province.

Deshpande - Registrar of a district who, in the peninsula, performed the same duties as the qanungo of the Mughal empire. The desmukh and the despande were to the district/pargana what the headman and patwari were to the village.

Farman (P) - Imperial Order.

Faujdar - An officer under the Mughals invested with the charge of police and had jurisdiction on all criminal matters.

Fusgee - A small duty levied at fairs and weekly markets on shroffs in money and on other dealers in kind.

Fusli, Fasli (from A. fasl or fasal) - The harvest year. Fasli 1210 (corresponds with 1800-1801, difference of 590 years. The Madras government fixed its commencement to the 12th July.

Gola, Golla - Supplier of milk or sheep.

Gomasta, Gomastah, Gomashtah (P) - An agent, steward, or representative.

Gosayeen, Gossain - Follower of Shiva Order, corresponding in many ways with the Bairages among Vaishnavas, many of them officiate as priests in the temple of Shiva; one of the most respectable of the Hindu orders.

Grama-maniyam - A term used to denote an in 'am enjoyed by the whole community of mirasidars, hereditary function aries - palegars, zamindars, faujdars, patels, karnams, kattubadis etc.

In'am, Enam, Enawm (A) - Present, gift gratuity, favour. Grants of land free of rent; or assignments of the government's share of the produce of a portion of land, for the support of religious establishments and priests and for charitable purposes; also to revenue officers, and the public servants of a village.

Jagir (P) - A tenure in which the public revenue of a given tract of land were made over to a servant of the state together with the powers required to enable him to collect and appropriate such revenue, and administer the general government of the assigned territory. The assignment could be conditional or unconditional.

Jamabandi - The annual settlement of revenue accounts in an estate, village, or district.

Jodi - Quit rent. It implies that in 'am granted was not absolutely revenue-free but subject to the payment of a jodi or salami. Generally a half or quarter of the gross value of the produce was paid as jodi.

Kach'hari - Court of justice; also the public office where the revenues were paid, and other business, respective the revenue, transacted.

Kamil, Kamal (A = Perfect) - The full assessment of land.

Kani,

Kani-atchi

Kaniadsi (T) - Hereditary rights; Taniil term for meeras. Also, a particular measure of land (fixed in 1800 at 1.32 acres).

Kapu - A cultivating class of sudras; they may even stand for leading agriculturists of the place if not village officials; enjoying considerable status in the society.

Karkoon - A clerk acting as an assistant to Sheristadar and Tehsildar.

Karnam, Kurnam
Curnam (K) - A village accountant also Patwari, Shenbogue, Kulkarni, Menon etc.

Kattubadis - Peons or militia men employed by the palegars for military service, performed police and revenue duties. Grama Kattubadis, village servants and peons, performed service through out the year; Jangi Kattubadis, called for service on emergent occasion. In practice both the classes performed revenue and police duties indiscriminately, as occasion required.

Kattubadi In'ams - Land grants, in 'ams granted to kattubadis.

Kaval - Protection money.

Kavalgar,
Kavalkaran
(Tam.) - Watchman, police incharge for the protection of the village.

Kaveli russom - Protection money. Fee or perquisite of a Kavalgar.

Khairati - In 'ams granted to Muslims for charitable purposes. Secular in 'ams.

Kiladar, Qiladar - Fort commandant.

Kist, Qist, Kisht - Stated payment, instalment of land revenue

Kotwal - Chief officer of police.

Kunbhava - Marathi term for the hereditary right in land.

Langarkhana - In'am for the support of an alms- house, a place where food and alms were distributed to the poor under the Muha,madam government.

Mahal (A) - Places, districts or sources of, or yielding revenue, particularly of a territorial nature, sometimes encom-passed the entire pargana.

Malkiyat,
Milkiyat - The usual term for property in land; ownership.

Marah - An allowance in grain upon each plough or upon the quantity of seed sown.

Mawas - Recalcitrant areas or villages which refused to pay taxes unless forced to do so, same as zor-talab.

Meeras,

Miras (A) - 'Permanent hereditary property'; 'heritage, succession, patrimony'; hereditary right whether to land; office, or other resource. According to one of the judgements, 'without the consent of the proprietors of the soil, the collector has no authority to deliver any part of these lands to other persons.'

Moolvies - A small duty on goods passing through the areas concerned.

Mu'afi - (lit exempted from the payment of revenue). Revenue-free holdings; any revenue-free grant may be called mu'afi; no condition of military service was attached.

Muqaddam (A) - Head rayat or principal man of a village, looked after the affairs of it and collected the revenues within his jurisdiction, same as patel.

Munshee, - Clerk conducting the collector's correspondence Moonshi with Indian revenue servants.

Nandavanam - In 'am for the maintenance of a garden, the flowers of which were appropriated to the use of a pagoda or of the village community.

Nirrlu Pandal - Same as 'Tannir Pandal'.

Padikaval - Right of policing.

Pagoda - Currency in which ac were usually maintained in most parts of south India. The most prevalent Pagodas were Star Pagoda and Cantaroy Pagoda. The former was usually understood to be equal to 3½ rupees and latter equal to 3 rupees. Also an idol temple.

Palaiyam, Pollam (T)	-	An estate, district, war camp, fortress held by a palegar.
Panam	-	A gold coin (equal to 100 kasu, copper coins).
Pargana	-	Administrative division or sub-division of a sarkar, a tract of country consisting of varying number of tappas or villages.
Patasala	-	In 'ams for the- support of schools where the Vedas were taught.
Patel. (K)	-	Headman, munsif of a village, titled variously in local usage in south India (pedda rayat, reddi, kapu, dora, kadim, mirasdar, naidu, nattamkar, monigar, maniakkaren, etc. The adjective pedda was often prefixed there to)
Patta, Pattah	-	A lease, deed, contract, receipt, or official document of certification; specifically, a document specifying the land revenue due from a piece of land or a. person, terms and conditions on which the lands were held. Lands which were thus granted were called patta lands.
Peon	-	A footman, a foot soldier, an inferior officer or servant employed in revenue. police, or judicial duties, sometimes armed with a sword and shield.
Peshkash, Peshkush (P)	-	Offering or tribute paid to a superior or the government. The payment of the peshkash was a mark of subordination to the superior.
Pradhani	-	Technically the finance minister, principally engaged in directing the collection of revenue and its expenditure.
Ra'iyati	-	Peasant-held villages or against zamindar villages The term should not be with rayatwari villages.
Raja	-	King, prince, chieftain, nobleman.

Rayat, Ryat,
Raiyat (A) - A subject, but especially denotes a cultivator, farmer or peasant, whether under a zamindar or, as in Bombay and most of Madras, independent in his relation to the revenue authority. It is in the latter capacity that he is usually referred to here.

Rayalaseema - The word in Telugu means the 'seema' or the country of the Rayalu, the title assumed by the Vijayanagar rulers especially belonging to Aravidu dynasty.

Rayatwari,
Ryotwari,
Raiyetwari - A settlement made by government immediately with the rayats without intermediary renters or zamindars-also Kuiwar settlement

Riaya, Ri'aya - All cultivating families paying revenues to the state.

Russom,
Russoom,
Rusum (A) Customs, customary, commissions, gratuities, fees, perquisites.

Shares of the crops and ready- money payments received by public officers, as perquisites attached to their situations.

Sahukar,
Sowkar, Saukar, - Merchant, banker, a money lender.
Savukar (H) Sahukar

Sanad,
Sunnud (A) - A patent, charter, or wiitten authority for holding either land or office.

Sanad-i-milkiyat
-i-istimrar - Title-deed of perpetual ownership.

Sarkar, Sirkar,		
Circar	-	Part of a suba; the government.
Sheristadar	-	Keeper of records, revenue accou ntant of a district who checked the accounts of the regular village accountants. Head ministerial officer of a court, hence a head native officer in district head quarters.
Shroff	-	A banker or money-lender.
Shrotriyam		A general term for all favourably assessed villages held by Brahmans.
Suba,		
Subah (A)	-	A province.
Subedar (P)	-	The Viceroy or Governor of a province. In 18th century this office had become hereditary. The title also used to designate a military officer.
Swastiyam (T)	-	Term for ownership right among Bralunans.
Talaiyari,		
Talliari,		
Tallari (T)	-	The village watchman, guard, messenger, etc. also called Totie.
Taluk,		
Talook,		
Taluq (A)	-	An administrative subdivision of a district.
Taluqdar	-	Holder of a taiuq.
Tankhah,		
Tankhwa (P)	-	Salary, wages.
Tannir Pandal	-	In 'am for the service of maintaining a water pandal where water and buttermilk were distributed to travellers during the hot season.
Tehsildar,		
Tahsildar (H)	-	A native revenue official, in Mardas Presidency, the chief administrative officer of a taluk.
Tope	-	The term means a grove of trees, properly of trees that bear fruit, as mango, tamarind,

		coconut etc. Lands occupied by such trees and held free of assessment were treated as in 'ams.
Totie, Totier	-	A caste of Telugu cultivators, village policemen, also guard the crops and assisted in measuring them.
Urani	-	In 'ams for maintaining in repair the village ponds for supplying drinking water.
Vakil, Vakeel, Wakil (A)	-	Authorized representative, attorney, pleader, lawyer.
Vees	-	Equal to 1.75 to 2 acres.
Waqf (Plural Auqaf)	-	Beneficiaries of such grants were institutions/individuals on collective basis; for the maintenance of religious shrines, tombs and madrasas, - for their repairs, as also for the subsistance of their 'staff' and for charities disbursed through them. Though reckoned as heritable proprietary estates in nature, in practice it was always subject to alteration or even confiscation by the state.
Waratanah	-	An allowance in money paid by husbandmen on ploughs and by tradesmen on houses, shops and looms.
Watan Jagir	-	Hereditary land or area held by the ruling class families, also place of residence.
Zamindar (P)	-	Broadly speaking, the holders (of the rights over the produced) of the land. This term implied a range of highly variegated dominant rural classes and was inclusive of the so-called rajas who had an 'autonomus' control over the territories under their jurisdiction
Zamindaran-i-zor-talab	-	Zamindars or palegars who would not pay the revenues unless demanded forcibly.

Zamindary	-	An office or jurisdiction of a zamindar. A settlement recognizing zamindars as hereditary proprietors of the soil.
Zillah	-	An administrative district.

Dr. Kalaignar Thiru M. Karunanidhi Endowment Lectures, Madras University, Madras, 7th, 10th, 11th April, 1995

Lecture I

The Palegars

Respected Professor R. Balasubramanian, Distinguished Scholars, Ladies and Gentlemen:

I am extremely indebted to the Department of Politics and Public Administration, Madras University for inviting me to deliver the prestigious Dr. Kalaignar Thiru M. Karunanidhi Endowment Lectures, thus, giving me an opportunity to share with you my ides and thoughts on some aspects of the history of South India. I am fully conscious of my limitations for delivering lectures before this august forum, which has had the privilege of having most eminent scholars in the past. It is only long association with the history of South India and the affection of my colleagues over here, which has given me this honour and privilege.

The choice of the subject, 'Landed Elites in Upheaval—Forms and Contents of Resistance by the Palegars' looks rather ambitious. It is a study of an important institution, the Palegars, and two different phases of their resistance in South India especially the Ceded Districts, an important part of the erstwhile Madras Presidency, during the period 1800-1847.

While discussing the palegar institution, it has been emphasized that it cannot or rather should not be looked into in isolation. An attempt has been made to draw parallels between the different categories of the zamindars of the Mughal empire and the palegars. The first phase of their resistance was part of the chain of such spontaneous resistance against the English, which had continued almost right since the very inception of the English as a political power in India. It was mainly aimed at seeking greater share in the power over, and thus in the revenue of, their region. The latter resistance, though part of the same chain, was the first against the British policy towards one of the most sensitive and traditionally adorable institutions, the *in'am* lands. Their seeming intention to subvert the traditional social order aroused the hostility of the conservative element, the general people, the *in'amdars,* the country people and villagers of different social status and, as such, gave strength to the already disgruntled elements, the palegars.

It is a technical and difficult subject and any reliance on fragmentary source material would be unsystematic and easily liable to misinterpretation. The important source material consulted includes—the relevant records, both manuscript and printed, contemporary and near-contemporary, preserved in the Tamil Nadu State Archives, Madras; OML, Madras; Andhra Pradesh State Archives, Hyderabad; Karnataka Secretariat Library, Vidhan Sauda, Bangalore; National Archives of India, New Delhi; and in Collectorate/Deputy Commissioner Offices and Tehsildar Offices of the Cuddapah, Kurnool, Anantapur and Bellary. It is notwithstanding the fact that extremely valuable contributions made by different scholars to the study of the palegars have been an immense inspiration and guiding force to me.

I propose to entitle my three lectures as **'The Palegars': Two Phases of the Palegar Resistance and British Policy'**: and **'Comparative Study of the Nature of Palegar Resistance'.**

"It is absurd to say that we must never extend our dominions though we see a state falling to pieces, and every surrounding one seizing a portion of its territory," wrote Thomas Munro to his father.[1] It is a very apt comment on the period of political turmoil and turbulation through which India had been passing during the eighteenth century and the intentions of the English East India Company which wanted to take fullest advantage of the prevailing situations. In order to achieve their objectives, as the history shows, the Governor Generals like Warren Hastings, Cornwallis, John Shore Wellesley etc. would not pay any heed to the directives from the home government. It is quite well known that the Act of 1784 had Stated that 'the pursuit of schemes of conquest was repugnant to the honour and policy of the British nation', yet the unsettled state of India was a sufficient excuse for them to go to war.[2] It cannot however, be completely ruled out that perhaps both the home government and the East India Company were hands in glove.

In contrast to the mid-eighteenth century, during the second half of the same century, as both empire and commerce grew, imperical interests in Indian affairs became valuable, politically and financially, both for the Company and the British nation. The history, particularly of the last quarter of the eighteenth and first quarter of the nineteenth centuries, shows that though the meaning of imperialism depended on the goals, intellect, and intensity of interest among individuals and groups involved in India, they had a unanimity on their elemental conviction that British power must be maintained in India.[3]

The East India Company certainly bad a very active imperial interest in India as its very survival as a commercial corporation depended on the preservation of the Indian empire. The imperial attitudes of the Company were directly derived from their political and economic stakes in India. The Governors and officials in India, besides reflecting the imperial sentiment of aristocratic Britain and the mercantile interests of the Company, had a personal stake in the permanence of British power in India. As such, there was a general agreement that British power must be preserved in India.[4]

The acquisition of Bengal, Bihar and Orissa may be considered 'in a great measure accidental,'[5] but after this success the diplomacy and the military force of the English East India Company had given them 'such a superiority over the ever-changing, tottering governments of the native Princes' that 'by watching times and opportunities, and making a prudent and vigorous use' of their resources had extended their dominion without much danger and expense.[6]

It was the same diplomacy and the military force, which accounts for their acquisition of the areas known as the 'Ceded Districts' and their policy towards the palegars.

All the English reports pertaining to the early nineteenth century have written about the existence of as many as 80 palegars and their about 30,000 armed retainers in the Ceded Districts at the time of their cession to the East India Company in 1800.[7] The palegars in the Ceded Districts were semi-independent revenue collectors and, of smaller pretensions, police-in-aid of the revenue collector. They held possession of an extent of territory, maintained an armed establishment and headed the administration. During the course of the time the palegars had started assuming the role of petty sovereigns and claimed hereditary proprietary rights over their estates called *palaiyam*. However, they could not legally and properly be called landlords. As a matter of fact, only a few of them, who were really men of local weight and standing, could claim to have become landlords, and held the *sanad-i-milkiyat-i-istimrar* or title deed of perpetual ownership.[8] They did not buy or sell land, or dispose it of by gift, as it was an *in'am* and resumable at will. The grants bestowed on the palegars were given for a specific purpose and entitled them the share of the produce payable as rent, though in theory they got 'complete ownership of the soil', including, according to the mode of expression, all its property both above and below ground. The grant given away in this manner could be a piece of land, a village or villages, and sometime *taluk* or *taluks*. Since all grants were resumable at pleasure, and as all persons were every moment liable to be deprived of their estates, technically they could never be considered as landlords. Their primary duty was to render military service and pay *peshkash* for the land, they possessed, to the sovereign.[9] The concentration of these two important duties, together with the rights arising therefrom, accounted not only for the vast influence of the palegars but also both politically and economically, a potential danger in the Ceded Districts. As such, it had become quite imperative for the Company's officials to go deep in the background of the palegars and to come out with the ways and means to check their growing power if the English had to establish an effective political power and introduce administrative measures in the Ceded Districts.

Different writers, chroniclers, travellers, English records, and archaeological survey reports pertaining to various parts of South India, have commented on the palegars and the *palaiyam* system, their origin, nature and working as an institution.

The origin of the *palaiyam* and palegar system have been by and large, unanimously attributed to Vishvanatha Nayaka of Madura (A.D. 1529-1564) and his *dalavay*[10] and *pradhani*[11] Ariyanatha. Some of the sources, however, do point out that the system did exist even prior to the Nayakship of Vishvanatha and accepting the prevalent system he improved upon it, thereby making it basis for his effective administration. In this regard the

Mackenzie Manuscripts[12] are of considerable importance for not only the above viewpoint but also for understanding the origin and history of the palegars and the *palaiyams.*

The numerous manuscripts make it amply clear that the *palaiyam* system was in existence much before the rule of the Nayaks of Madura.[13] C.S. Srinivasachari has also opined that the elements of the system were in existence even before the spread of Vijayanagar sway into the Tamil country.[14] However, it is quite possible that before their rule the system was perhaps in a rudimentary shape and the Nayaks sufficiently systematized and organized it on a rational basis.

It is also amply clear from the *Mackenzie Manuscripts* that the prominent palegars holding *palaiyams* with hereditary rights were *boyas, gollas* and dominant peasants like *kapus* and *reddis.*[15] It is also borne out by the 14th Century inscriptions that the *boyas* of this region, referred to as *boyaviharadesha* (the land where *boyas* roam) and *boyavidu* (the land of *boyas*), were already powerful in early medieval times.[16] With their economic prosperity and rise in social hierarchy some of the *boyas,* from around 12th century A.D., also made gifts of cattle, money and land to the temples. Subsequently they began to give up the suffix 'Boya' and adopted the ones like 'Nayak', 'Reddi', Nayudi', 'Nedu' and Raju'.[17] The *gollas* too emerged as palegars and legitimized themselves as Yadavas like those of Kunkanur, Dudikonda and Maddikera. For instance, palegar Madapa Naidu, great-grandson of palegar Mallikarjuna Naidu received (A.D. 1570-72) from Tirumal Naidu of Aravidu dynasty 29 villages as *jagirs,* as was also bestowed with regal insignia. Palegar Madapa Naidu belonged to the *karisena golla* lineage but in his genealogical records he claimed descent from the *yadavas,* and the *chandravamsha* (moon born).[18]

The *Mackenzie Manuscripts* speak of the creation of seventy-twc *palaiyams* by the new rulers of Madura, each under a palegar who was responsible for its defence. It is hard to believe that the number of the *palaiyams* created in the beginning remained the same or this system remained confined to Madura alone. Considering the clamant demands of Vishvanatha's multitudious followers, and the arduous nature of the improvements to be effected in the region, the number must have started increasing immediately after the inception of this institution. The later references show that the system had even travelled to other parts of south India also.[19]

In the *palaiyam* system the possession of land, though on military tenure, not only provided a palegar dignified status but was also the basis of the system. However, it is notwithstanding the fact that in due course of time the position and the grant, legally and illegally, had become hereditary. The palegars were given complete powers of police and judicial administration. In return for the assignments of lands and other administrative powers, a palegar was required to fulfil certain obligations to the imperial house. The obligations included the payment of annual *peshkash* or tribte (in theory one-third of their income from land), maintenance of a standing army (again in theory, with another third part of his income), which his master would require in case of war and, attendance at the Imperial Court on important and ceremonial occasions. In practice, however, they would enjoy more than one-third of their revenues. At the same time, for loyal and public services remissions in the tribute were also given, sometimes even to the extent of whole amount. My research shows, it was not always necessary that a palegar would be given a land grant for the maintenance of the army. He could meet this expenditure partly from the land grant and partly from the cash payment made by the government or wholly by the cash payment made by the government. Sometimes part of the land grant was converted into a *in'am* land or the *vice versa*. In some cases if the land grant was not sufficient to meet the requirement, he was appointed *kavalgar* (police incharge for the protection of the villages) of some neighbouring villages and *kaveli russom* (protection money) thus collected would meet the requirement of the army and *peshkash.* At times, the number of soldiers to be maintained was increased or decreased resulting into corresponding decrease or increase in the tribute. The tribute was sometimes increased or decreased even without decreasing or increasing the number of soldiers to be maintained. The service could be completely remitted and the tribute was increased or was supposed to pay the land revenue as per the assessment. Above all, in case of disloyalty or habitual non-payment of the tribute, a palegar could even be expelled. There is at least one reference, which shows that the grant given on military tenure would lapse if it was mortgaged to a *sahukar* against a loan taken from him.[20]

The institution as such and administrative, judicial and police rights of the palegars had close links with another old institution, also current during the Vijayanagar period and even after i.e., *kavalgars.* Whereas in the centrally administrated areas in the Vijayanagar empire, there existed three types of police (i) maintained by the state, (ii) maintained by the people, and (iii) special police at the capital, the provinces under the *Nayaks* and *Kavalgars* were remunerated by assignments of land for their maintenance. They themselves appointed *talaiyaris* (village police functionaries) for the village under them (usually one *talaiyari* for each village) who, in return for their services rendered, were paid both in kind and in cash, besides being granted land free of rent. In some places the villages sold the right of policing (called *padikaval*) to the *kavalgars.* In many an instance some local chieftains, especially the palegars, were assigned *padikaval* duties. Sometimes the grant of *kaval* rights was made to certain people as a reward for their services.[22] The protection money was also paid by the merchants, artisans, shepherds, fishermen, washermen and others.[23] As stated above, many palegars were assigned the duties of *kavalgars* and in many places the *kavalgars* also grew into palegars. T.V. Mahalingam has opined that the authority of the palegars was derived from *padikaval,* a right to income in return for the provision of protection over a village, or in some cases over a locality during the Vijayanagar period.[24] In due course of time, especially after 1564, not only many other categories of persons, Brahman immigrants, many Telugus, and other favoured agents in the new regime received official titles and the perquisites attached, but institutions of *kavalgar* had also started becoming hereditary.[25]

The *palaiyam* system was indigenous in origin and design and it would be wrong to align it with feudalism in medival Europe. The terminology of that peculiar socio-political system which arose in the Middle-ages in Europe has been very vaguely and carelessly applied to Indian institutions by many a writer. Some western or even Indian writers persist in calling as 'fiefs' even the assignments which were made to their officers by the different rulers of India, and the word feud is quite as freely and indiscriminately used. Some scholars, like Moreland, for instance, wrote that the use of feudal terminology of Europe to denote any institutions of India which might have a superficial or even partial resemblance with the former is highly inappropriate and misleading.[26]

The palegars were bound by the ties of military to the above chief or the king and held lands on *amaram* tenure i.e., military tenure.[27] They had no proprietary right over the land nor could they count on the cultivators as their serfs. They were to pay dues from their lands to this superior chief and were responsible for the supply of the stipulated number of foot and horse soldiers. In case the stipulated service was not rendered, the *amarams* were resumed by the grantor.[28]

Indeed, several incidents of the *palaiyam* system and feudalism look so akin that they seem to have a common origin. For instance, the palegars also held the lands immediately or mediately of the suzerain in return for a fixed annual *peshkash* and the maintenance of stipulated military contingent. They also gave their lands to their subordinates on similar terms. It was these rather striking resemblances and common incidents, which have misled some writers into drawing an exact analogy between the two systems.

The *palaiyam* system was the result of the deliberate policy of the rulers in assigning territories on *amaran* tenure in return for military service and fixed financial contribution. This system linked together only a section of the population and its gradual expansion did not reach a high degree of perfection in Vijayanagar nor afterwards. Though in due course of time the office and the land grant had become hereditary yet they were still in theory as well as in practice under the suzerain power and could be expelled and their grants resumed. Moreover, the comparative independence they enjoyed within their territories provided them opportunities for waging wars against each other. At the same time, they would go even to the extent of defying the central authority if the rulers were inefficient.

In the aftermath of the victory at the battle of Talikota, the frontier of Golconda extended to the south below the Krishna river which included the major portion of the Ceded Districts. For the maintenance of order as well as collection of taxes in the newly acquired territories the services of most of the palegars cum *kavalgars* or palegars and *kavalgars* were recognized. This was with or without changing their service conditions.[29] At the same time, apart from creating new palegars/*kavalgars,* some who were already in service in different capacity were appointed as palegars/*kavalgars.* The research shows, as many as twenty three old ones were retained, sixteen were fresh appointments and six were those who had earlier served in different capacity.[30] The Golconda sultans, in brief, tried to obtain, at a minimal cost, the consolidating and continuing protection of the newly acquired southern frontier. It was, merely, a policy of compromises and accommodations. The conquerors, in fact, 'formed a political elite in a complex society of pre-existing social and political institutions'.[31]

The battle of Talikota provided Bijapur rulers also ample scope for expansion in the Karnatak and some of the areas namely, Adoni, Penukonda, Harpanahalli, Jenimulla, Bellary, Doodikonda, Dewankonda, Anantapur, Raydroog etc., which later on formed the parts of the Ceded Districts.[32] They, however, had to face resistance from the palegars and other chiefs of the region. These chiefs were temporarily prevailed upon to pay annual tribute. Being equally determined to preserve their newly achieved independence, these chiefs/palegars would yield and pay tribute only when pressed hard by the Bijapur army. The result was that the Bijapur army had to conqueror again and again the same territory.[33]

Apart from the resistance provided by the chiefs/palegars to both Golconda and Bijapur, the artificial league between the Muslim powers also could not last long and broke almost immediately after their victory over the Vijayanagar empire. The internecine quarrels were resumed with greater fury than ever before and had rather provided additional ground for hostilities. The inability to establish effective political ascendancy and central authority upon the erstwhile Vijayanagar areas on the part of the Muslim sultans resulted into unchecked rise of the local chiefs and the palegars. These chieftains who, in fact, exercised sovereign rights within their jurisdiction, were never adequately dealt with during this period.[34]

During the Mughal campaigns in the Deccan from 1685 onwards these chiefs/palegars constituted a body of officers available for military and administrative service, and were politically and economically dominant in different parts of Golconda and the areas under study. Many of them were discharged or their service remitted or reduced; amount of *peshkash* was increased; land grants were reduced or resumed; and some were replaced by Muslim officers. Some of those who were retained were employed as auxiliaries hired by the Mughals in the Maratha war in the Karnatak.[35] Some of the redundant chiefs turned to banditry. There were widespread turbulences as well as plundering by the local chiefs. Moreover, as is evident from almost every contemporary source, the distress in the region from famine and epidemic had also resulted into political troubles. A large number of disturbances were due to high prices and food shortages as *zamindars* and bandits looted stocks of grain and money from the merchants and other wealthy persons.[36] As such, it is scarcely surprising that public opinion in these areas continued to exhibit a dislike of the new regime. These circumstances gave sufficient impetus to the palegars to defy the central authority and their status attained permanancy. William Thackeray in his *Report* has rightly emphasised that the palegars found in the Ceded Districts at the time of their cession were generally those who rose between 1565 and the time of Aurangzeb.[37]

During the eighteenth century the areas under study were the scene of fierce struggle for power between the Cuddapah Nawabs, Marathas, Nizam, Haider Ali and later Tipu Sultan. All these powers tried to establish their suzerainty over different chiefs/ palegars and tried to collect *peshkash/chauth* from them. The palegars paid the tribute not according to any fixed principles, but according to the power of the government to enforce it. The management and administration of their *palaiyam,* and the control of their subjects, were left entirely to the palegars. They were constantly at war either with each other for the extension of their respective power or against the sovereign power.

It can safely be argued that the rise of the palegars and turning of the Ceded Districts into a state of deterioration and anarchy, was, by and large, because of the succession of inefficient governments and rapacity and weakness of the persons who were entrusted with their management.[38]

The palegar institution in the Ceded Districts, or for that matter in several other parts of South India, cannot or rather should not be looked into in isolation. It is necessary to see whether this type of institution existed only in this part of India or in other parts of contemporary India also, though with a different nomenclature. For that matter a peep into the period specially from Akbar down to the end of the 18th century, including the rise of the Sikh sardars in parts of the *subahs* of Delhi and Punjab, cannot be avoided and certain parallels can be drawn between the different categories of *zamindars* of the Mughal empire and the palegars. In this regard reference may be made to the scholarly contributions made and the conclusions drawn by B.R. Grover,[39] S. Nurul Hasan[40] and Irfan Habib,[41] the pioneers on the Mughal economic history. The above writings highlight that despite a clash of interests, the Mughal empire was fundamentally dependent on the cooperation and support of the each of the broadly three categories of the *zamindars*, namely the chieftains, the intermediary and the primary *zamindars*. Even though there were important regional differences, the nature of land rights in most parts of the country was basically similar.[42] The first category of the *zamindars*, namely the chieftains, were hereditary autonomous rulers of their territories. The Mughals in order to obtain from these chieftains the recognition of their overlordship, imposed on them the obligation to pay regular tribute/*peshkash* and render military assistance whenever called upon, and at the same time absorbed many of them in the imperial hierarchy and administrative machinery. They were also responsible for the maintenance of the law and order and the freedom of transit. Depending upon the circumstances and the number of soldiers to be maintained, apart from the hereditary dominions, called *watan jagirs*, they were also assigned *jagirs* in other area. The amount of *peshkash* was fixed on the basis of the actual production, data regarding the area under cultivation, the crop pattern, and the revenue realized. Moreover, they were also entitled to a share in the plunder while conducting compaigns on behalf of the empire. A chieftain, however, depended for his position on the goodwill of the emperor rather than on his inherent rights. The hereditary succession as well as his remunerations/*jagir* were both conditional upon the performance of the services to the state.[43] All this shows hardly and difference between the reasons and circumstances under which the institution of palegars came into existence and the position enjoyed by them.

The intermediary *zamindars* were those who collected the revenue from the primary *zamindars* and paid it to the imperial treasury, or to the *jagirdars,* or to the chieftains or in certain cases kept it themselves. This right was of intermediary nature and not a proprietary right, rather a right of service and a service obligation. They were also responsible for the maintenance of law and order. As remunerations they enjoyed various types of perquisites, like commissions, deductions, revenue free lands, cesses etc. Though usually the *zamindars* possessed hereditary rights, in a few cases they held their position on short-term contracts as well. In this category, apart from the class of *zamindars* who contracted with the state to realize the revenue of a given territory, *deshmukhs, desais deshpandes* and *muqaddams* etc. were included. Despite being hereditary an intermediary *zamindar* could not only be dismissed or transferred, the state reserved the right to interfere with his succession also.[44]

The primary *zamindars* for all practical purposes held proprietary rights over agricultural as well as habitational lands and carried on cultivation themselves, or with the help of hired labour. Those who would bring forest and waste under cultivation were also bestowed with the *zamindari* rights. A primary *zamindar* could be a *zamindar* of some area, a village or even several villages. The rights held by them were hereditary and alienable.[45]

It has to be clearly borne in mind that the above divisions of the *zamindars* during the Mughal period is a very broad one. There could be numerous divisions of the *zamindars* within these three broad categories. The main idea behind giving the position in the Mughal period is to pin-point similarities between the areas under discussion and the contemporary north India. In both the regions the existence of the various types of landed interests had been the result of long process of evolution spread over several centuries.

If the above broad division of the *zamindars* is applied in case of the palegars that existed in the Ceded Districts at the time of their cession to the English it could be argued that out of eighty palegars the ancestors of as many as thirty nine belonged to the category of chief *zamindars*/palegars right since the beginning of their career. They were assigned lands, supposed to maintain a contingent (big or small) and/or paid *peshkash*.[46] As many as twenty nine got their positions during the period of Vijayanagar empire; two during the period of Raja of Annagundi; six during the Golconda period, one during the Bijapur period; and one during the Cuddapah·Nawab's period.[47] The ancestors of eight palegars could be put in the category of intermediary *zamindars*. Two of them were initially *diwans* and two were *patels* while one had a few villages in *jagir* during the Vijayanagar period. One of them came into existence during the Golconda period and two during Aurangzeb's period. Three of them were recognised as chief *zamindars*/palegars during the Golconda period, one during Bijapur period; one during Aurangzeb's period; while three of them came to be recognized so by the time Marathas dominated the areas.[48] Two palegars were originally *dalavays* and one a *daffedar* during the Vijayanagar period, and one each got the recognition as chief *zamindar*/palegar during Bijapur, Golconda and Aurangzeb's period.[49] Out of fourteen originally primary *zamindars*, four became so during Vijayanagar, nine during Golconda and one during Aurangzeb's period. Two of them were recognized as chief *zamindars*/palegars during Golconda, four during Aurangzeb's period and one during Cuddapah Nawab's period, and while five tried to assume that role during Haider's period but were subdued and one remained practically satisfied with his positiion.[50] Eleven of the palegars were originally *kavalgars*, so appointed, seven during Vijayanagar, two during Golconda, one during Aurangzeb and one during Cuddapah Nawab's period. Four palegars were initially *taliarys*, and one was either a *taliary* or *kavalgar*, all the five appointed during the Vijayanagar empire. Out of these sixteen, six got the recognition as chief *zamindar*/palegar during Golconda, one during Bijapur, and three during Aurangzeb's period, while two assumed such role during Haider's and one during Tipu's period. Three of them were very petty or insignificant palegars.[51] The Table given below will make the position still clearer.

Table

S.No.	Palegar of	Original Appointment/ Recognition	Period	Period in which recognized As Palegar/ Chief Zamindar
1	2	3	4	5
A.				
1.	Raja of Annagundy	Raja	Vijayanagar	-
2.	Jenimulla	Palegar/Chief Zamindar	-do-	-
3.	Busvapur	-do-	-do-	-
4.	Pulalcherru	-do-	-do-	-
5.	Bollapally	-do-	-do-	-
6.	Neelagutla	-do-	-do-	-
7.	Niddamaddoddi	-do-	-do-	-
8.	Nosum	-do-	-do-	-
9.	Chitveyal	-do-	-do-	-
10.	Singapattan	-do-	-do-	-
11.	Bodyemenoor	-do-	-do-	-
12.	Talmurlah	-do-	-do-	-
13.	Pyapalli	-do-	-do-	-
14.	Sampilli	-do-	-do-	-
15.	Yerragunta Palaiyam	-do-	-do-	-
16.	Madanpalli	-do-	-do-	-
17.	Papypilli	-do-	-do-	-
18.	Rampicherlah	-do-	-do-	-
19.	Mullel	-do-	-do-	-
20.	Dudipalli	-do-	-do-	-
21.	Maddancherru	-do-	-do-	-
22.	Kokimti	-do-	-do-	-

23. Millacherroo	-do-	-do-	-
24. Wudiamunhi	-do-	-do-	-
25. Yagawamarapahgunta	-do-	-do-	-
26. Digawamarapahgunta	-do-	-do-	-
27. Sanyapanyni	-do-	-do-	-
28. Vimlah	-do-	-do-	-
29. Rattangery	-do-	-do-	-
B.			
1. Oapalur	Palegar/Chief Zamindar	Golconda	-
2. Marsellah	-do-	-do-	-
3. Talpool	-do-	-do-	-
4. Chintalguntah	-do-	-do-	-
5. Motguntlah	-do-	-do-	-
6. Jallalmundah	-do-	-do-	-
C.			
1. Dewankonda	-do-	Bijapur	-
D.			
1. Ghuttim	-do-	Raja of Annagundy	-
2. Butlapur	-do-	-do-	-
E.			
1. Nangangunta	Plegar/Chief Zamindar	Nawab of Cuddapah	-
F.			
1. Bellary	Diwan/ Intermediary Zamindar	Vijayanagar	Bijapur
2. Hundi Anantapur	-do-	-do-	Aurangzeb
3. Narsapur	Patel/ Intermediary Zamindar	-do-	Golconda

4. Whurpur	-do-	-do-	-do-
5. Muddikerah Mulla	Intermediary Zamindar	-do-	-do-
G.			
1. Kalupalli	-do-	Golconda	Marathas
H.			
1. Talpool Taluq	Intermediary Zamindar	Aurangzeb	-do-
2. Kadiri	-do-	-do-	-do-
I.			
1. Rayadroog	Dalvovy	Vijayanagar	Bijapura
2. Tutt	-do-	-do-	Golconda
3. Madicheroo	Daffedar	-do-	Aurangzeb
J.			
1. Owk	Primary Zamindar	-do-	Golconda
2. Tipradipalli	-do-	-do-	-do-
3. Tumalgundi	-do-	-do-	Cuddapah
4. Yellutlah	-do-	-do-	Haider Ali
K.			
1. Chuppalmurragu	Primary Zamindar	Golconda	Aurangzeb
2. Vencatadry	-do-	-do-	-do-
3. Woorlaguntah	-do-	-do-	-do-
4. Kullipundah	-do-	-do-	Cuddapah
5. Bvanmullah	-do-	-do-	Haider Ali
6. Rangangar *Palaiyam*	-do-	-do-	Aurangzeb
7. Yedamuneyn *Palaiyam*	-do-	-do-	Haider Ali
8. Nellamune *Palaiyam*	-do-	-do-	-do-
9. Moodiampaur	-do-	-do-	-do-
L.			
1. Rawoor	-do-	Aurangzeb	Cuddapah

M.			
1. Doodikonda	Kavalgar	Vijayanagar	Golconda
2. Pundikonda	-do-	-do-	-do-
3. Mutialpur	-do-	-do-	-do-
4. Shilliwar *Palaiyam*	-do-	-do-	-do-
5. Ganguichentlah	-do-	-do-	Aurangzeb
6. Noputnutlah	-do-	-do-	Petty Palegar
7. Nomutnutlah	-do-	-do-	-do-
N.			
1. Kotapalaiyam	-do-	Golconda	Haider Ali
2. Madaneyn *Palaiyam*	-do-	-do-	Tipu Sultan
O.			
1. Yellamundah	-do-	Aurangzeb	Haider Ali
P.			
1. Kapugunapalli	Kavalgar	Cuddapah	Petty Palegar
Q.			
1. Harpanahalli	Taliary	Vijayanagar	Bijapur
2. Kodikonda	-do-	-do-	Aurangzeb
3. Kapitral	-do-	-do-	-do-
4. Yerrawar *Palaiyam*	-do-	-do-	Golconda
R.			
1. Kamlapur	Kavalgar or Taliary	-do-	-do-

Another common feature amongst the different categories of the *zamindars,* in different parts of India during the medieval period, was that they were constantly struggling to enhance their position and tried to go up the ladder. In this attempt they frequently came into clash either with the state or the superior category of the *zamindar*. The chief *zamindar*/palegars would hardly miss an opportunity of taking advantage of the difficulties faced by the empire. In such circumstances they attempted to convert their *amaram* lands or the *jagirs* assigned outside their ancestral territories into hereditary ones, and would on occasion even assume independence. In case the state was unable to maintain its military pressure on the chiefs, the revolts became more frequent, as was the case in those parts of the Ceded Districts which came under the Nizam in 1792 and 1799.[52]

The different categories of the intermediary *zamindars* tried to improve their position in two ways. They would try to reduce the primary *zamindars* to the status of tenant-farmers or would try to go a step higher and become chieftains. They struggled and strived to appropriate a greater share of the revenue if not the whole of it, so that they could spend more on their armed contingents. Tipu Sultan must have faced similar difficulties from the *patels* that is why *Hukam Nama-i-Tipu Sultan* mentions about the strict instructions given to them.[53] There are innumerable references pertaining to the pàlegars and the *zamindars* in Mughal empire who would not pay the revenues unless demanded forcibly. Such *zamindars*/palegars could be put under the well-known category of the *zamindaran-i-zor-talab.* In order to achieve objective they frequently rose in rebellion either on their own, or along with their fellow brethren, or even joined hands with some of the chieftains who were already in revolt against the state.[54]

In the quest for a higher status, the primary *zamindars* were also not lagging behind and thus struggled to become intermediaries and then chiefs. In this process they frequently came into conflict with the superior *zamindars* and the state on the one hand and the peasantry on the other.

Some of the erstwhile high state officials, *kavalgars* and *taliaries,* taking advantage of the weak government and their military/police powers, also rose and were successful in getting the status of palegars.

The question for higher economic and political status and struggle for achieving that was also true, among others, in case of the Maratha chiefs and the Sikh sardars during 17th/18th centuries.[55]

References

1. Letter from Thomas Munro to his father, dated Trichangoor, 21 September 1798, Gleig, G.R., *The Life of Maj. Gen. Sir Thomas Munro, Bart and K.C.B Late Governor of Madras* (London, 1830), Vol. I, p. 203.
2. Carrington, C.E., *The British Overseas, Exploits of a Nation of Shopkeeprs: Part I (Making of the Empire),* (Cambridge—at the University Press, 2nd Edn., 1968), p. 181.
3. *Parliamentary Debates from the Year 1803...Forming a Continuation of the work entitled 'The Parliamentary History of England From the Earliest Period to the Year 1803'*—Published under the superintendance of T.C. Hansard, 22 November, 1803-28 February 1830, 41 vols., London, XXIV, p. 412, 23 January, 1784 (Hereafter, *Hansard*).
4. Bearce, George D., *British Attitudes Towards India 1784-1858* (Oxford University Press, 1961), pp. 34-37. *East India Company, Debates at the East India House in the General Court of the Proprietors of East India Stocks* (8 vols., London, 1813-44), ii, pp. 17-50. David Scott, *Correspondence,* 2 Vols., (London, 1951), ii, p. 39.
5. 'Result of Lord Wellesley's Administration', Col. George Chesney, *Indian Polity,* Ist Edn., 1868, p. 32, quoted in Owen, Sidney J. (ed.), *A Selection From the Despatches, Treaties and Other Papers of Marquess Wellesley, During His Government of India* (Oxford, 1877), p. 812.
6. Letters from Thomas Munro to his father, dated 21 September 1798, *op. cit.*, p. 203.
7. TNSA, *Poligars: Col. Munro's Report Regarding the Poligars in the Ceded Districts, with a Memorandum of Poligars 1801-1802;* ASO (D) Vol. 62 (21), Letter from Thomas Munro to William Petrie, President and Members of the Board of Revenue, 20 March, 1802; Letters from Thomas Munro to the Board of Revenue, 12 August 1801, *Selections from the Old Records of Bellary District 1800-1807,* ASO (D) Vol. 72, Letter from Thomas Munro to Josiah Webbe, Chief Secretary to Government, 12 July 1807. *Selections from the Records of Bellary District—Political, Revenue and Agricultural Matters 1800-1857,* ASO (D) Vol. 73, Letter from Thomas Munro to William Patrie, 22 July, 1801. Mahalingam, T.V. (ed.), *Mackenzie Manuscripts, Summaries of the Historical Manuscripts in the Mackenzie Collection,* ii, (Madras, 1976), Different Manuscripts, *Fifth Report,* pp. 499-530.
8. Baden-Powell, B.H., *The Land Systems of British India,* 3 Vols. (Oxford, 1892, Reprint, Delhi, 1974), III, pp. 15, 19.
9. TNSA, ASO (D), Vol. 72, *Selections from the Old Records of the Bellary District 1800-1807,* Letter from Thomas Munro to William Petrie, President of the Board of Revenue, dated Anantapur, 25 August, 1805.
10. *Dalavay* was the principal officer of the Vijayanagar empire, combining in himself the control of all civil and military adminstration. It was, as a matter of fact, the fusion of the functions of a *mantri* i.e., chief minister and a *senapati* i.e.,

Commander-in-chief. The Jesuit letters have indicated his great power under Queen-Regent Mangammal (1689-1706 A.D.). He was entrusted with the entire administration, of which he was absolute master. He was thought to be greatest master that ever governed Madura. 'Letter of Father Peter Martin to Father Le Gobien, Aoor, in the kingdom of Madura, 11 December 1700'. John Lockman, *Travels of the Jesuits,* being translations from the *Letters edifiantes etc. curieuses, ecrites des Missions etrangers, par les Missionaires de la Compagnies de Jesus* (20 March 1762), 2 Vols., I, p. 461, reproduced in Aiyar, R. Sathyanatha, *History of the Nayaks of Madura,* edited by S, Krishnaswami Aiyangar (Oxford University Press, 1924), (hereafter *Nayaks of Madura*), pp. 235-36, 308. J.H. Nelson in his *The Madura Country: A Manual* (Madras: Asylum Press, 1868), p. 145, does not give much importance to this official and has described his functions as 'merely advisory'.

11. *Pradhani* was technically the finance minister, principally engaged in directing the collection of revenue and its expenditure. However, it seems that in the absence of *Dalavay* from the capital he acted as 'the governor or rather the despot of the whole kingdom.' *Nayaks of Madura,* p. 237.

12. Mahalingam, T.V. (ed.), *Mackenzie Manuscripts: Summaries of the Historical Manuscripts in the Mackenzie Collection,* 2 Vols. (Madras University, Vol. I, 1972 and Vol. II, 1976), (hereafter *Mackenzie Manuscripts*).

13. *Ibid.* I, Manuscript No. 1, section 3, pp. 6-7, 'Genealogical Account of the Poligar of Naduvakuricci in the Cola Country.

    Manuscript No.2, section 6, pp. 21-23, 'Genealogical Account of Kulappa Nayaka Poligar of Nallakata (Nilakkuttai) in the Dindigul District'.

    Manuscript No.3, section 2, p. 27, 'Account of the Poligar of Kakkuvadi in Kongunadu'.

    Manuscript No.3, section 5, p. 29, 'Account of Vanava Rayagauda Poligar (Vanaraya Kaundan Poligar) of the Samattur Palaiyappattu'.

    Manuscript No.3, section 6, pp. 29-30, 'Account of Debnik Poligar of Pullaksi (Deva Nayaka Poligar of Pollachi) in the Dharmapura District.'

14. Srinivasachari, C.S., 'The Polegar System—Its Development and Decay', *Journal of Madras University,* Vol. III, 1955, p. 272.

15. *Mackenzie Manuscripts*, Maddikera kaifiyat, Manuscript 168, No. 1201; Aspari Kaifiyat, Manuscript, 168, No. 1201; aspari Kaifiyat, 123, No. 923; Nandyal Kaifiyat, Manuscript 110, No. 793; Rollamadugu Kaifiyat, Manuscript, 108, No. 738.

16. For details see, B.S.L. Hanumantha Rao, 'The Boyas in Andhra History', Journal of *Andhra Historical Research Society,* 38, 1983-84, pp. 77-91.

17. M.L.K. Murthy, 'Environment, Royal Policy and Social Formation in the Eastern Ghats South India, A.D. 1000-1500', Presidential Address, Historical Archaeology, Epigraphy and Numismatics Section, *Indian History Congress,* 53rd session, Warangal, 1992-93, pp. 615-631.

18. *Mackenzie Manuscript*, Kunkanur Kaifiyat, Manuscript, 123, No. 928; Dundikonda Kaifiyat, Manuscript, 146, No. 1149; Maddikera Kaifiyat, Manuscript, 116, No. 855.

19. *Mackenzie Manuscript*, I, Manuscript No. 2, Section 6, 7, No. 36; II, No. 105-136. *Nayaks of Madura*, pp. 58-59.

20. *Mackenzie Manuscript*, I, Introduction, pp. xxxi-xxxii; II, Manuscript No. 118, p. 128. Mahalingam, T.V., *Administration and Social Life Under Vijayanagar*, 2nd edn. Part I (Madras, 1969), p. 138. Taylor W. (ed.), *Oriental Historical Manuscripts*, 2 Vols. (Madras, 1862), II, pp. 160-68. Venkatasubramanian, T.K., *op. cit.*, pp. 10-11; *Nayaks of Madura*, p. 59. *Narrative of Domingo Paes*, the Portuguese Traveller (written, probably, A.D. 1535-37) reproduced in Sewell, Robert, *A Forgotten Empire: Vijayanagar* (New Delhi: Publication Division, 1962), pp. 228-78 and 279-376.

21. About the functions of the police, see The Persian Ambassador, Abdur Razzak's account in Elliot, H.M. and Dowson, J., *The History of India, As Told by Its Own Historians*, 8 Vols. (London, 1866-1877), IV, p. 112. Fernao Nuniz's account in Sewell, Robert, *op. cit.*, p. 361.

22. *Annual Report on Epigraphy* (South India) for the years 1887-1944/45 (Madras, 1887-1955), para 240 of 1912 and para 368 of 1914. *Inscriptions in the Pudukkottai State* (tr.) English by K.R. Srinivasa Iyer. Parts I and II (1941, 1946), II, para 751.

23. Ludden, David, *Peasant History in South India* (Oxford University Press, 1989), p. 73. M.L.K. Murthy, *op. cit.*, p. 625.

24. Mahalingam, T.V., *South Indian Policy* (Madras: Madras University, 1967), pp. 247-49.

25. Ludden, David, *op. cit.*, p. 72. Mahalingam, T.V., *Administration and Social Life Under Vijayanagar*, I, *op. cit.*, p. 139.

26. Moreland, W.H., 'Feudalism (?) in the Moslem Kingdom of Delhi', *Journal of Indian History*, Vol. VII, Part I, 1938, Saran, P., *Studies in Medieval Indian History*.

27. *Amaram* means land or revenue granted by a chief to his retainers for military service (*Tamil Lexicon, op. cit.*, I, p. 102). McClean, C.D. defines an *amaram* grant as a grant of land to the prince or poligar on condition of service generally military or police (*Manual of the Administration of Madras Presidency*, III, (Madras, 1885), pp. 24, 352.

28. *Inscriptions in the Pudukkottai State, op. cit.*, para 743. 'Narrative of Domingos Paes' and 'Chronicle of Fernao Nuninz', Sewell, Robert, *op. cit.*, pp. 269-70 and p. 354 respectively. Barbose, Duarte, *An Account of the Countries Bordering on the Indian Ocean and Their Inhabitants Written by Duarte Barbose and Completed About 1518*, tr. With notes etc. by Longworth Dames, 2 Vols. (London, 1918), I, p. 209.

29. *Mackenzie Manuscripts*, esp. no. 109, section 1-13.

30. Sherwani, H.K., 'The Region of Abdul'l Qutab Shah (1626-1672): Economic Aspects I', *Journal of Indian History*, XLII (August 1964), pp. 443-70; II, XLV (December 1967), pp. 115-60. *Fifth Report*, pp. 499-530.

31. Richards, J.F., *Mughal Administration in Golconda* (Oxford, 1975), pp. 30-34.

32. *Mackenzie Manuscripts,* No. 105, Section 6 and No. 209, Section 1-3. *Tarikh-i-Farishtah* by Muhammad Qasim, Hindu Shah, Farishtah, English translation, Briggs, John, *History of the Rise of the Mohamedan Power in India,* 4 vols. (Calcutta, 1910), II, pp. 40-46.
33. *Tarikh-i-Farishtah, op. cit.,* II, pp. 47, 56-57; Verma, D.C., *History of Bijapur, op. cit.,* pp. 126-36.
34. *Tarikh-i-Sultan Muhammad Qutb Shahi,* account of Golconda inserted in, Briggs, John, *op. cit.,* III, pp. 416-17. Brackenbury, C.P., *Madras District Gazetteer—Cuddapah* (Madras, 1917), p. 38.
35. Sarkar, Jadunath, *History of Aurangzeb,* 5 Vols. (Calcutta, 1912-30), IV, pp. 350-352. Richards, J.F., 'The Hyderabad Karnatik, 1687-1707', in *Modern Asian Studies,* IX, (1975), pp. 241-60. Ali, M. Athar, *The Mughal Nobility Under Aurangzeb* (Aligarh, 1966), pp. 216-71. *Fifth Report,* pp. 499-530.
36. TNSA, *Records of Fort St. George: Diary and Consultation Books,* Diary of 1687. *Record of Fort St. George: Despatches to England,* Different letters from and letters to Fort St. George pertaining to years 1687-1688. Raychaudhuri, Tapan, *Jan Company in Coromandel: 1605-1690.* Verhandelingen van het Koninklijk Institut voor Taal-Land-en Volkenkunde, Vol. XXXVIII (The Hague, 1962), pp. 68-74. *Mackenzie Manuscripts,* No. 144, pp. 224-28.
37. TNSA, ASO (D), Vol. 66, *Report of William Thackerary,* dated 8 September 1807.
38. TNSA, *Selections From the Records of Bellary District, Political, Revenue and Agricultural Matters,* ASO (D), Vol. 73, Munto to Josiah Webbe, dated 18 March 1801; Letter from George Garrow to Munro, dated 8 December 1801.
39. Grover, B.R., 'Nature of Land Rights in Mughal India', *The Indian Economic and Social History Review,* Vol. I, No. I, 1963, pp. 1-23. 'Nature of *Dehat-i-Taaluqa* (zamindari villages) and the Evolution of the *Taaluqdari* System During Mughal Age', *The Indian Economic and Social History Review,* Vol. II, No. 2, 1965, pp. 166-77 and II, No. 3, 1965, pp. 259-288. 'Elements of Continuity and Change in Land Ownership and Rights from the Mughal Age to the Early British Administration in India', Presidential Address, Medieval Indian Section, *Indian History Congress,* 37th session, Calicut, 1976. 'The Position of *Desai* in the *Pargana* Administration of Subah Gujarat under the Mughals', *Indian History Congress,* 1961, pp. 150-55.
40. S. Nurul Hasan, 'The Position of the Zamindars in the Mughal Empire', *IESHR,* IV, pp. 107-19, also in Frykenberg, Robert Eric (ed.), *Land Control and Social Structure in Indian History* (New Delhi, 1979), pp. 17-31 (under the title 'Zamindars under the Mughals'); 'Three Studies of the Zamindari System', *Medieval India: A Miscellany* (Bombay, 1968), pp. 233-39; 'Aspects of Zamindari System in Deccan', *IHC,* 1969, pp. 262-66; *Thoughts on Agrarian Relations in Mughal India* (New Delhi, 1973, rpt. 1983).
41. Habib, Irfan, *Agrarian System of Mughal India* (Bombay, 1963).
42. For a discussion on various types of land rights see, Grover, B.R. 'Nature of Land Rights', *op. cit.*

43. S. Nurul Hasan, *Thoughts in Agrarian Relations...*, *op. cit.*, p. 28; 'Position of the Zamindars...', *op. cit.*, Grover, B.R., 'Nature of *Dehat-i-Taaluqa...*, *op. cit.*, Khan, A.R., *Chieftains in the Mughal Empire During the Reign of Akbar* (Simla, 1977), p. 6-7.

44. S. Nurul Hasan, *Thoughts on Agrarian Relations*, *op. cit.*, pp. 29-33; 'Position of the Zamindars', *op. cit.*, Grover, B.R., 'Nature of *Dehat-i-Talluqa*', *op. cit.*, Position of Desai', *op. cit.*, Dua, J.C., 'Comparative Position of the Village Headmen During the Early British Rule in the Punjab and the Madras Presidency', *Punjab History Conference*, Patiala, 23rd Session, 1987; also in Dua, J.C., *Agrarian System in South India (Some Aspects)*, (Delhi, 1990), pp. 123-36.

45. S. Nurul Hasan, 'Position of the Zamindars', *op. cit.*

46. In this regard see Grover, B.R., 'Elements of Continuity and Change... ', *op. cit.*

47. See Table.

48. *Ibid.*

49. *Ibid.*

50. *Ibid.*

51. *Ibid.*

52. TNSA, Munro to William Petrie, dated 20 March 1802, *op. cit.*, ASO (D), Vol. 72, Thomas Munro to the Secretary of the Committee of Police, dated 10 September 1806. Report of William Thackeray, dated 8 September 1807, *op. cit.*, Munro to Josiah Webbe, dated 18 March 1801, *op. cit.*, S. Nurul Hasan, 'Zamindar Under the Mughals', *op. cit.*, Grover, B.R., 'Nature of Dehat-i-Talluqa...', *op. cit.*

53. APSA, *Hukamnana-i-Tipu Sultan* (Persian), dated 1206 *Fasli*, Clause No. 11 (I am grateful to Professor B.R. Grover for deciphering and interpreting relevant portions for me). Dua, J.C., 'The Position and Role of the Village Headman in the Village Administration of the Ceded Districts During the First Quarterly of the 19th Century', in Dua, J.C., *Agrarian System in South India*, *op. cit.*, pp. 83-106.

54. *Supplementary Report of the Special Committee*, *op. cit.*, p. 39, Raju, A. Sarada, *Economic Conditions in the Madras Presidency, 1800-1850*, (University of Madras, 1941), p. 45. S. Nurul Hasan, 'Zamindars Under the Mughals', *op. cit.*

55. Dua, J.C., *British Historigraphy: Eighteen Century Punjab* (New Delhi, 1992), pp. 95-96, 214n. Grover, B.R., 'An Analysis of the Contemporary Revenue Documents and Correspondence Pertaining to Patiala Chieftainship (*Zamindari*) during the later half of the 18th Century', *Punjab Past and Present*, XXIV-I, April 1990, pp. 196-233.

Lecture II

Two Phases of Palegar Resistance and British Policy

First Phase

Thomas Munro, the Principal Collector of the Ceded Districts (1800-1807), on entering the districts, found a general rebellion of the palegars. Every one of these palegars, howsoever, petty his territory, kept up a mimic court and a small standing army of permanently appointed soldiers aided by a militia of relative of these soldiers. As already explained in the previous lecture, these palegars had attained their position in a number of ways. Some of these had originally been servants of government, or renters of districts or had received their villages at first in *in'am* as personal allowance for the support of their rank, and had revolted in times of disturbances. Some of these palegars had received their villages at the usual revenue, both as a personal *jagir*, and for the service of a body of horse and foot soldiers. Some were commanders of body of soldiers, paid in cash not by *jagir*, then after being absolved from military service became renters of some villages, and finally by holding those areas for a number of years during the times of confusion, came at last to be denominated as *zamindars*/palegars substituting the term *peshkash* for that of revenue. Some were merely renters assessed to the full *kamil* (*i.e.*, full assessment of land), and ultimately grew into palegars. In some parts of the Ceded Districts, almost every head of a village, favoured by the natural strength of the area became a palegar. All these people took advantage of the weakness of the government, withheld the revenue to support the troops, and enjoyed all the forms of a prince of an extensive territory.[1] Almost every village was exposed to their ravages and the Ceded Districts were nothing more than a nest of 'robbers'. Here it may be pointed out that describing the palegars as 'robbers' 'maraudars', 'predatory bands' and their activities as 'depredations', 'pillaging', 'highway robbery' is a concept usually used from the imperialist viewpoint. Whenever the revolting *zamindars* or chiefs realized the revenue of a particular area after occupation, from the imperialist angle it was described as plunder, loot, pillage etc. Same is true about the Mughal description about the Marathas, and the British description, amongst the other chiefs, about the palegars in the South India and the Sikh sardars in the Punjab during the eighteenth century.[2]

The palegars maintained large bodies of armed followers (called 'peons' in the English reports) for the performance of their police duties in addition to those who acted as their armies. These armed followers could be compared with those maintained by the chief *zamindars* in north India and the Northern Circars. They consisted of (i) those paid entirely in cash, had no other means of living, and they were the least numerous; (ii) those who enjoyed service lands, but who, being composed of *rayats* who rented other lands, regarded their *in'ams*, only a secondary object; and (iii) who confined themselves to the cultivation of their *in'ams*. However, each one of them received *bhatta*, when called out beyond the limits of their villages. The usual allowance of land, as revealed by the survey and investigations conducted by Thomas Munro, to a common armed follower, in the Ceded Districts, appears to have been a field valued at six pagodas annual rent. The village headmen, who used to maintain armed followers, were allowed a piece of land from 9 to 24 pagodas rent for parties of 10, 50 or 100 as the case might be. It is also learnt that the palegars in general kept up 6 persons for every 100 Star Pagodas of gross revenue in their respective *palaiyams*. Since every one of them had relations able to bear arms and was required to bring them into the field in cases of emergency, the palegars were enabled, whenever necessary, to assemble a much larger force than their fixed establishment amounted to.[3]

The armed followers maintained by the palegars were also known by the term *kattubadis*. Functionally speaking, the *kattubadis* were of two types—*grama kattubadis* and *jangi kattubadis*. The former were purely village servants and were required to perform service throughout the year. The latter were called out for service on emergent occasions. The lands granted to them came under the title *kattubadi in'ams* and were subject to quit rent.[4]

The contemporary records show that though practically whole of the areas under the Ceded Districts were directly or indirectly affected by the activities of the palegars, their menace was not identical in all the areas. For instance, in Cuddapah, despite the fact, that the palegars did not hold great proportion of the lands, were greater in number, were very powerful and had on the account produced great resistance. The palegars, especially, of Chitvel, Nossam, Narasapur, Vimla and Talpoor, had been repeatedly in resistance particularly during a decade before and after the cession of the areas and were considered to be most powerful in the Ceded Districts. In Gurramkonda, the palegars had even defied the authority of Tipu Sultan, and, though expelled, had been collecting large annual contributions from their old possessions. The palegars of Rayadrug and Harpanahalli, who, during the course of time, had acquired considerable territory, and that of Owke, Chitvel and Anantapur whose ancestors had held high positions during the Vijayanagar period, were regarded by the different powers, who ruled over the areas under study, as holding an independent authority. However, the degree of their resistance was not always the same. Contrary to the palegars of other portions of the Ceded Districts, especially the Cuddapah area, as already referred to, where all those who had survived all the changes of government which had followed so quickly upon one another's heels frequently required regular troops to reduce them to order, in the Anantapur area none of the chieftains were formidable enough. Of the four palegars, except the one of Kamalapur who was obstreperous, those of Anantapur, Nadimidoddi and Talmurlah were not at all troublesome.[5] However, in Adoni, not far from Anantapur, the position was quite alarming.

The disturbed political condition and proper land revenue collections would not normally coexist. The case of Ceded Districts was in no way different and the palegars' activities had their bearing on the income of the government from the then greatest source of earning. The first attempt of the Company to collect the revenue from this newly acquired territory provoked a general resistance of the palegars.

"War, famine and bad management", remarked William Thackeray, "all appear to have combined to reduce the Ceded Districts, but the rebellions of the Polligars seem to have been the major cause of the decline of the revenue."[6] Moreover, in the areas which, either wholly or partly, composed of the palegars' possessions, the government was bound to appoint extra manpower, and receive less revenue than in those which were 'properly Sirkars'.[7]

The authorities in Madras and Bengal were in favour of divesting the palegars of their military and political powers and wanted them to be treated as *zamindars* under the principles of the Permanent Settlement of Bengal. Different reports and incidents are eloquent to the fact that the Company's position with regard to the palegars had already become set even before Thomas Munro assumed control of the Ceded Districts. During the second half of the eighteenth century when palegars were considered as a formidable obstacle to the consolidation of its authority in the far south, the Company was engaged in a high cost long series of compaigns against them, which had culminated in the widespread uprising of 1800-01.[8] This must have produced some circumspection within the Madras government by the time Munro took over. The Governor General, Lord Wellesley, the Court of Directors and the Madras Board of Revenue all had come to favour more leniency and 'progressive approach to the improvement of the administration of Poligar affairs'. In addition to this sagacious and discreet reconsideration of policy, the Madras Government was also instructed that the Bengal regulations were to be established in Madras and in 'poligar countries', and they (palegars) were 'to receive the permanent possession of their lands on zamindary tenure'.[9]

However, there were not many voices in the Madras Presidency that had any good to say of palegars, and the persons who had closely watched their activities and had to actually deal with them, e.g. Thomas Munro, Thackeray and even Madras Board of Revenue were hardly enthusiastic about Wellesley's instructions that these chiefs were to be vested with permanent rights in their lands.

Thomas Munro, however, had a different way of looking at the things and the claims made by the palegars, backed, of course, by the authorities in Madras and Bengal. His understanding of the nature of landownership and rights of the *zamindars* in India in general and Madras Presidency in particular was perhaps much better than his contemporaries and near contemporaries. The people usually termed *zamindars*, he opined, were not more land owners than the *in'amdars*. The appellation of *zamindars* among the natives of India, he felt, comprehended every person who held land and discharged the duties of a civil officer down to the village *taliary* and also all palegars and rajas.[10]

Thomas Munro was not in favour of using force right away. If the palegars were wise enough to submit, they could be permitted to retain their estates in which they collected rent, part of which was to be passed on the government as land revenue. Another condition that he wanted to impose was that they must give up their power of justice, their armed retainers, and all the tattered shreds of sovereignty they had pulled around themselves.

In order to put the onus of action by the government on the palegars themselves and avoid any risk of mass reaction by them, Munro issued a Public Notification on 15 April 1801. This Notification banned garrisoning of any fort by the palegars, *jagirdars, zamindars, patels* or even *rayats*. They were asked to desist from maintaining the body of armed men and extorting money from the inhabitants either in the shape of *kaveli russom* or under any other pretence. Major-General Dugald Campbell, who had been appointed to command the troops in the Ceded Districts and to assist Thomas Munro to restore peace, was empowered to trial, and punish with death any person convicted of any of the above crimes.

Munro also proposed to raise the level of *peshkash* to the highest previously ever demanded by the Nawabs of Cuddapah or Haider Ali or by the Nizam's regime. At this high pitch of demand, Munro reasoned to Webbe, palegars would not be in a position to pay their troops, and maintain their military capacity and also pay the tribute to the Company. They could, however, maintain the troops only by withholding their payments to the Company. When, as he expected, they defaulted on the payments, they could be deposed and expelled legally. He concluded his proposal with the remarks, in a letter to Webbe, 'I am convinced that it is possible to expell them all and to hang the great part of them. The idea was also to change the *peshkash,* or customary tribute, into a land rent assessed at nearly the same rate as that on the sarkar land.[11] This would not only change the very character of the palegar institution and the nature of the palegars' relations with the government, but would also revert back to the original positions those palegars who had earlier changed their revenues to *peshkash.* Since this measure would considerably deprive the palegars of their hitherto enjoyed, power and position, opposition was bound to be there, but Munro was confident of overcoming that by perseverance.

As regards the troops employed by the palegars, government had several options before it. Their services could be dispensed with; even while being out of service they could be allowed to retain their *in'ams* by granting them *sanad* in the name of the Company; or their services could be transferred to the government.

It may be pointed out that identical policy in regard to all the three types of armed personnels,[12] referred earlier, was not approved/allowed by the government, All those who were paid cash remunerations were straight away recommended to be enlisted in the government battalions. The other two categories who were paid in the form of *in'am* lands were permitted to hold their lands on easy terms or on the payment of a stipulated quit rent, and were to be considered militia in times of necessity.

A Proclamation (1801) was issued directing the palegars and others to surrender the said arms within a period of three months from the time of issuing the proclamation. The palegars were, however, authorised to retain a certain number of pikesmen (number to be determined by the Governor in Council upon the representation of the palegars) for the purpose of maintaining their pomp and state. The pikesmen, thus allowed, were to be registered in the *kach'hari* of the collector, and the pikes to be stamped by the collector.

The practical aspect of different ideas and the policies proposed showed that Thomas Munro, in the first instance, maintained a *status quo* in regard to the lands held by the palegars. As planned, he raised the *peshkash* too high to render it impossible for them to pay and at the same time maintain their troops. He knew it fully well that even if they consented to pay, that would be without any serious intention of doing so.[13]

The experience of a few months proved Munro's hunch correct that the palegars would not pay the requisite amount and that little was to be got from them without compulsion. Most of them even refused to come to the *kach'hari* unless they were allowed to settle the amount of their *peshkash* in their own way.[14] Obviously, most of them had large amount of balances against their names. It was against Munro's policy to act leniently with the defaulters and wanted 'to insist upon their becoming answerable for the whole assessment' of their *palaiyams.*[15] The result was that some of the most powerful and several inferior chiefs who fell into the arrears, resisted, refused to come to the *kach'hari*, and/or took up arms, forces were sent against them and were captured, imprisoned, expelled, and/or were pensioned off. There is a long list of palegars who showed resistance against the government.[16]

The action taken against the above palegars did not mean that their power had been completely finished. Not only many more of them had not still been apprehended, even those who had apparently accepted the terms dictated by the English were likely to endeavour to recover their lost power.

Major General Campbell, who had been appointed the commanding officer to try and punish all rebels and all others opposing the English establishment in the Ceded Districts, was, meanwhile, given additional powers to try and award capital punishment on conviction to all such palegars.[17]

Encouraged by the success of the early steps taken to curb the power of the palegars in an attempt to establish Company's authority throughout the Ceded Districts completely and not to leave a set of turbulent chiefs in a condition to oppose it, Thomas Munro applied/got approved a set of new measures which were both more effective and economical. Acting on the suggestion of the Chief Secretary, communicated to him through General Campbell, he appreciated the expediency of inducing the Nizam to consent to allow part of the subsidiary force stationed at Raichur to move to Bellary.[18] He further suggested that the local militia should be chiefly stationed in the palegar areas. The appointment of the local militia was regularized and the subordinate collectors were asked to appoint the Companies as per the requirements of different areas.[19]

Despite making sufficiently elaborate arrangements to deal with the palegars, a stiff opposition from them could not be ruled out. All these chieftains had, by then, emerged to be quite defiant by nature. Even earlier, as already discussed, though 'bound certainly to pay to the ruling power tribute and military contingent, for most part, had generally managed not only to evade these payments, but in many instances to exact tribute from other smaller chiefs.' The earlier wars had, of course, impoverished them and reduced their power but they had escaped annihilation by yielding allegiance to each new master. They, as a matter of fact, had seen so many successive governments that they did not expect the British rule to be a permanent one. They, therefore, endeavoured 'as much as possible to evade its demands.' It was, however, difficult to escape from the 'clutches' of the 'new master', 'who would not be content with mere professions of allegiance, unless at the same time he received the practical proof of it in the shape of regularly- paid rent'.[20]

Thomas Munro dealt with several other palegars,[21] during his tenure as Principal Collector of the Ceded Districts, but the intention is to give only a few samples rather than giving the details about each and every palegar. In nutshell, it may be mentioned that in 1807, when Munro left, the palegars had been thus disposed off:[22]

i)	Pensioned	2
ii)	Holding a *jagir*	1
iii)	Residing on their estates but deprived of authority	23
iv)	Managing their own estates	40
v)	Expelled by force	6
vi)	In confinement	8

	Total	80

None of the above categories had been given a free hand in his *palaiyam*. All those who were residing on or managing their estates were entitled only to a portion of the revenues as pensions or remunerations. The families of those expelled or in confinement were also given some pensions.

The policy of Munro's military action and the seizure of different palegars led to a great controversy and protracted correspondence involving the Principal Collector, Madras Government and the Court of Directors. The Court of Directors were not convinced by the reasons given by Munro for the proceedings taken against different palegars. They felt that the only principle upon which Munro had based his action was that it was 'absolutely necessary to the establishment of anything like a regular authority in the Ceded Districts that no opportunity should be lost of expelling the Polligars.' They even directed that Thomas Munro 'be removed from his situation of collectors in those Districts (Ceded Districts), and that he be not employed in any Revenue Post in future, which the violent and mistaken principles of his conduct seem to render him unqualified to fill in a way that would be satisfactory to our feelings.[23]

It seems there was either a lack of proper coordination between the English authorities in Madras and the Court of Directors or the former did not care much about the orders and instructions from England, or were more enthusiastic about the establishment of the Company's authority in India.

Thomas Munro, in his defence, argued with the Board of Revenue (in a letter to be forwarded to the Court of Directors)[24] that for carrying into effect the government's instructions to establish their authority and in view of the state of the Ceded Districts in 1801,[25] the reduction of the palegars had become essential. However, it seems that the Board of Revenue 'quietly pocketed the increased revenues, which were the result of Munro's (as he was charged) "disingenuous and ill-considered policy", and to have made up their minds to say nothing about it. In 1807 when Munro resigned his post of Principal Collector and proceeded home on leave, he received a handsome acknowledgement by the Madras Government.

A careful study of the pension register maintained in the *taluq* office indicates that the columns 'Hereditary' and 'Not Hereditary' were left blank. It seems that either Munro wanted to play safe and did not want to commit whether the pension was hereditary or otherwise, or the government wanted to grant pensions to different palegars on different conditions. As far as the second contention is concerned, it is found, for example, that the Ghattum palegar and the Nossum palegars were sanctioned the pensions on the condition that 'the pension should depend entirely upon poligars continuing to reside at such place as the Collector may direct.'[26] Similarly, Baswapur palegar would get pension 'during good behaviour.'[27] The Register prepared by Robert Charles Ross, Collector of Cuddapah, in 1814 mentioned an additional remark on the subject. He wrote, "in the column of hereditary added—during good behaviour to lineal descendents only". This matter became a subject of discussion in 1822 when the Chitvel family petitioned for the continuation of the pension after the demise of the then incumbent. The Board of Revenue expressly stated, on the authority of Collector Ross, that the pensions were hereditary.[28] This matter once again became a topic of discussion in 1830. Incidentally, it again pertained to the Chitvel palegar, of course, linked with another thirty-six cases of the same type. The Board of Revenue asked Robertson, Collector of Bellary and Dalzall, Collector of Cuddapah about the nature of the land grants or pensions granted to the palegars. The Collector of Bellary observed that he could not discover that any actual pledge had any time been given to the parties that these allowances were to be hereditary. However, he quoted the example of Nossum palegar, whose mother, after the death of the incumbent, had been allowed by Thomas Munro to draw full allowances during her life. It was done on the plea that if decided otherwise, 'it would naturally exert a distrust among the Poligars that their lands or pensions would not descent to their children'. The Collector of Cuddapah simply narrated the above quoted example of Ross. The Board recommended the pensions to be hereditary but decided that any share of the pension, if given to the sister of deceased, would lapse on her death.[29] As such, it can be safely accepted that the pensions granted were to be enjoyed by the grantee and his heirs both in the male and female lines during good behaviour, and were liable to resumption on the family becoming extinct.[30] It was also clarified that the continuance of the pension depended on the pleasure of government and could not be claimed as a matter of right. In case of a lapse by death, the pension would be resumed *protempore* and the case reported for the orders of government.[31] In 1843 a suggestion to pay some money in lump sum in lieu of regular pension was turned down by the Governor General in Council on the plea that 'the payment of money, by way of redemption would soon be forgotten', while the abolition of pension 'would be remembered forever.'[32]

The descendants of the palegars continued to receive small allowances as pensions from the Government of India. In 1928, there were only ten such cases who received pensions in Bellary district.[33] On a visit to Cuddapah *tehsildar* office in 1969, it was found that some representatives were still receiving pensions.

The post Munro scenario of the Ceded Districts was comparatively much more peaceful and had only a few incidents of general interest. The only incident which could be termed as an incident of palegar resistance, took place in 1816 when a descendent of the dispossessed palegars of Koilkuntla and Nossum attempted to excite a general resistance.

Second Phase

The palegar resistance in the Ceded Districts was practically non-existent for nearly four decades after Thomas Munro's departure in 1807. It was in the year 1846 that the areas under study once again witnessed a major resistance from the palegars which incidently had much larger mass base covering different sections of the society, It is, however, by no means the intention to suggest that the palegars had suddenly turned into a happy lot and had no grouse against the East India Company during the intermittent years.

The successors of the palegars with whom Thomas Munro had made settlements had been, because the enormous divisions in the pensions and allowances, reduced to comparatively indigent circumstances. The loss of rank, influence and power coupled with meagre monetary allowance had made them a discontented lot. They would even draw a comparison between the rank and affluence of their ancestors and their own impoverished circumstances and unexalted condition in life. That is a different matter that perhaps the paucity of resources and manpower deterred them from revolting against the English.

This period of nearly four decades, especially the post-1813 period, was also full of active steps, on the part of the East India Company, taken towards the transformation of Indian society and culture. The more conservatives amongst the English administrators maintained that Indian civilization was different from European civilization. Opposing any programme of rapid modernization, they favoured the introduction of reforms very cautiously and gradually lest it should produce a violent reaction in the country. The things started taking a radical change due to the influence of Mill, Munro, Malcolm, Elphinston, Metcalf, Bentinck and above all with the coming of reforming Whigs in power in England after 1830. Despite their influence, the English policy continued to be imperialistic and exploitative favouring only those reformist measures which came within the framework of easier and more thoroughgoing exploitation of India's resources, One of the things that came into their accepted framework was the attempt to discontinue/fully tax the revenue free or favourably taxed grants, known as *in'am* lands in south, which had been, in some form or the other, in existence since the ancient times$_0$ Even persons like Raja Rammohan Roy, who was in league with the introduction of many a social and religious reform and was against priestly domination in the society had protested against the attempts to impose taxes on such grants.[34] However, the Regulation XXXI of 1802, the orders of 1825, the Regulation IV of 1831 extended by the Acts XXXI of 1836 and XXXIII of 1838, and the Minute of Consulation, 26 April 1845 clearly indicate the British intentions and policy towards one of the most important aspects of economic/ agrarian administration, the *in'am* lands.[35]

Without going into a detailed exposition on the origin and nature of the *in'am*, it could be roughly defined as a gift or benefaction conferred by a superior to an inferior person or institution. It was the custom to grant assignments of land revenue or at favourable revenue for all kinds of purposes like payment to troops, civil officers, maintenance and support of temples/mosques etc. and their servants, charitable institutions and reward for public services.[36]

In order to get familiarized with the *in'am* lands, it becomes essential to give a brief resume of such holdings. 'A descriptive list of the *in'am* tenures of the Madras Presidency' submitted to the Government on 30 October 1869, contained more than 400 separate categories of *in'am*.[37] Most of these *in'ams* were defined or described as land holdings either wholly free or partially taxed.

The East India Company's administrators alleged that a new phenomenon had started emerging in the grant of *in'am* lands during the period of anarchy, which preceded the English rule. They wrote, "the power of granting *in'ams* was assumed by various petty chiefs, officers of Government, and others, who alienated the revenues to a considerable extent. There is good reason to suppose that a large extent of land was granted as a *in'am* during this period by the parties who had not even the shadow of authority to make such alienation."[38] It seems to be too generalized a statement as the categories of the persons mentioned above had, though qualified, rights to bestow *in'ams* especially when they had assumed the role of a prince and the period was politically disturbed. The study of the pre-British system, in brief, shows that the *zamindars* and other assignees, both Hindus and Muslims, enjoyed transferable rights and could grant even hereditary revenue free grants. At the same time it may be pointed out, "The *malkiyat* rights of the assignees for the revenues and the land ownership rights of the self-cultivating *riaya* co-existed. In case an assignee tried to interfere with the latter's rights, his assignment was liable to be transferred."[39] As such, if there was deviation, it was not in the assignment of *in'am* lands by the *zamindars*/palegars etc., it was in the interference of the *riaya's* ownership rights. The English had their own interpretations and tried to act accordingly.

Instituting an inquiry at a very early date of their administration, the Company passed the Regulation XXXI of 1802 'to try the validity of the titles of the persons holding, or claiming to hold, lands exempted from the payment of revenue under grants not being *Badshahi* or royal grants.'[40] Despite a proposal put forward by the government that the *in'ams* be 'resumed and money payments substituted' the general result was that exempted lands were not only interfered with during the early surveys, the government of the day, following the custom of the country, also 'adopted the practice of rewarding meritorious services by grants of *jagirs,* and thus many villages were alienated either in perpetuity or for a stated number of lives'.[41] The practice of remunerating the village *patels* and *karnams* by land grants was also continued, though on new conditions.[42]

The practice of granting *jagirs* gradually fell into disuse after the orders from the Court of Directors, dated respectively 2 July 1822 and 27 May 1829. However, nothing was done in regard to the investigation of *in'am* tenures. Meanwhile, in 1825 orders were issued and a special establishment was sanctioned for that purpose in Bellary, but these measures were not put into practice. By Regulation IV of 1831, afterwards extended by Acts XXXI of 1836 and XXXIII of 1838 the *adalats* were prohibited from taking cognizance of claims the personal or hereditary grants of money or of land revenue whether conferred by the English government or made earlier by 'Native Governments' and confirmed or continued by the Company, except with the special permission of government.

Notwithstanding these legislative measures, neither the transfer nor lapses of *in'ams* were subjected to scrutiny as they occurred. In fact, no active measures were taken to vindicate the law until 1845, when the government issued orders strictly prohibiting local officers from continuing *in'ams* on the occurrence of lapses, and directing that each case should be reported for their orders through the Board of Revenue. This was followed in the next year (16 March 1846) by a proclamation notifying that adoptions involving inheritance to *in'am* lands should not be recognized unless reported at least six months before the death of the party making adoption.[43]

The policy initiated as an aftermath of the proclamation (16 March 1846) had the worst impact on two of the heretofore, discussed categories of the *in'ams*. These were *kattubadi in'ams* and the *bhatta-vritti in'ams*. It not only involved serious disputes but also proved to be the immediate cause of resistance against the East India Company in 1846.[44]

The *bhatta-vritti* and *Khairati* (if belonging to Muslims) *in'ams* had been in existence since the cession of the Ceded Districts to the Company. Thomas Munro had directed his surveyors that all sundry *in'ams* having no specific designation, under which they could be classed, should be entered, if belonging to Hindus, as '*Bhatta-vritti*', and if to the Muslims, as *Khairati*.[45] These *in'ams* were in the beginning bracketed together as *Dharmadayam* or secular, as distinguished from *Devadayam* or religious grants.[46]

The *bhatta-vritti in'ams* in the Ceded District were quite extensive, revenue-free landed tenures, held by different classes, but generally by Brahmins, as is implied by the term, which means 'For the support of Brahmins.' The *khairati in'ams* were of less than a whole village and were not service lands or granted on some specific account. The value of *bhatta-vritti in'ams* was much more than the *khairati* and were valued approximately at six lakhs rupees as per the survey assessment. The real annual value was, however, much less, as the lands were not all cultivated, and those cultivated were usually taken by the 'Circar' *rayats* on terms lower than the assessment. It was in reality a great assistance to the *rayats*, and in consequence a source of general prosperity to the area.[47]

The *bhatta-vritti in'amdars* were a large body of native gentry, many of them possessing considerable estates, comprising lands in many different villages, while others had but small holdings. Some of them were in the public service, others were engaged in commerce; but a great number lived on their properties, and subsisted on the production and rents of them, They had held their estates since the cession of the areas as private property, having perfect liberty to alienate them by gift or sale. They had confidence in the good faith of the British Government. They were sure that though no new grants would be made, no changes would be made in regard to old tenures.[48]

In 1845, the Board of Revenue declared the *bhatta-vritti in'ams* to be of the nature of charitable allowances mentioned in clause 2, Regulation IV of 1831. The Board prohibited any transfer of them by gift, or sale. These instructions were strictly acted upon, Accordingly, when an *in'amdar* died, his lands were attached immediately, and his family even when he left sons, were kept in a state of anxiety for months, When the order for continuing the *in'am* arrived, (if such was the order), the heir was informed that he would receive the estate of his ancestors not as his hereditary right, but as the bounty of government, and for his life only. The people were generally ignorant about the Regulations enacted by the government, and learnt its intentions only from the enforcement of orders by the local officers, They lost confidence in the permanency of anything, and would commonly say, "in what can we now trust" and, "in what respect is the Company's Government better than former Governments".

The *kattubadis* had received a special guarantee from Thomas Munro on behalf of the government that their *in'ams* would be continued to them hereditary during good behaviour and on condition of their yielding to the Company's government same services, which they had formerly been giving to the certain palegars.[49] Certain political motives, however, could not be denied behind the continuation of their hereditary *in'ams* and allowances as that was done to buy peace and to keep them quiet. Thomas Munro, vide his letter dated 10 April 1806, had agreed to maintain *status-quo* in the *in'ams* enjoyed by the *kattubadis* to save the Ceded Districts, especially the Cuddapah district, from the state of anarchy.[50] These measures were entirely successful in accomplishing the desired object. There are numerous documents to prove the hereditary nature of the *kattubadi imams.*[51]

The comparative change in the political scene between 1800 and 1845-46 cannot be denied. With the lapse of more than four decades the English had acquired vast administrative experience, political authority and military power. They had attained better position to suppress the armed and recalcitrant elements, if present, rather more easily and effectively. Besides, they would not hesitate in deviating from the position and policy adopted not only by the former Indian rulers but even by the earlier English administrators, in a bigger way.[52] What else could explain the policy initiated by the English government in December 1845? The policy was to retain only such number of *kattubadis* as was required in the village; to remove the rest, if they were willing (?), to other villages in the same *taluk* where there were few or none; to resume their *in'am* lands and to give fresh grants of waste land, according to the minimum standard of remuneration, in the villages of their posting; their appointments as well as the land grants were not to be hereditary and were subject to readjustments after their death; and all the remaining *kattubadi in'ams* were to be resumed on the death of the existing incumbents. However, their heirs could retain the lands if they chose to pay the full assessment.[53]

Accordingly, in Cuddapah alone the *in'ams* of 1396 *kattubadis* were to be resumed on the death of then possessors; 239 *kattubadis* were to be removed to other villages with their own consent (?); and the *in'ams* of 1695 *kattubadis* worth, as per the survey assessment, Rs. 74,895-15-10 were to be reduced. Incidently, excepting two, all the deceased *kattubadis* had left sons, brothers, or nephews, male heirs, entitled to succeed to their land. These incidents were directly connected with the insurrections that took place soon in the most adversely affected areas.[54]

The *bhatta-vritti* and *kattubadi in'amdars*, though agitated, could not give vent to their feelings unless they had an acceptable leadership who could unite them under his banner. The leadership was provided by another discontented youngman, Narasimha Reddy, a scion of two prominent and extensive erstwhile palegars of Oyelwada and Nossum *palaiyams* (both in Koilkuntla taluk then in Cuddapah and now in Kurnool district A. P.). Narasimha Reddy was the grandson in the male line to Oyelwada *palaiyam* and on his mother's side to Nossum *palaiyam*. Pedda Mulla Reddy (father of Narasimha Reddy) and his brother Chinna Mulla Reddy resisted the English authority and took refuge in Hyderabad territory where they remained for nearly 8 years. When they presented themselves before Chaplin, the Collector of Cuddapah, and solicited a pension, they were granted a monthly allowance of Rs. 70/-, i.e., Rs. 35/- to each. This amount of pension was quite inadequate to support them in a suitable manner and altogether very trifling in comparison with the revenues of their *palaiyam*, lately resumed.

Meanwhile both Pedda Mulla Reddy and Chinna Mulla Reddy had also died. Whereas the latter's pension of Rs. 35/- p.m. was continued to his widow, the former's pension was divided amongst his three sons — Kumara Mulla Reddy, Vurda Reddy and Narasinha Reddy. The three brothers advanced their claims for the continuance to them of the Nossum pension on the plea of their relationship to the original grantee, which was, however, rejected (1831).[55]

While his two elder brothers acquiesced in the decision given by the English government and uniformly manifested their submission to authorities, Narasimha Reddy was unable to reconcile himself to his straitened circumstances. The consequent poverty and indigence of his mature years, compared with the state and affluence of his childhood, had no doubt rankled in his mind. The different reasons given by various English reports for his ultimate armed resistance, the consensus is that he had both heard of and seen 'insurrections when protracted for some time ending in a compromise.'[56] He even thought of proceeding to Cuddapah and make a representation to the Collector regarding his circumstances and motives,' but was persuaded by the *kattubadis* to the extreme step.[57] Incidently most of the resumptions of *in'ams* had taken place in different villages of Koilkuntla taluk.

The sources indicate two prominent reasons as to why the *kattubadis* looked towards Narasimha Reddy as their leader. One, most of the *kattubadis* who ultimately joined him in the armed resistance, indiscriminately all were the descendants of the dependents and retainers of Narasimha Reddy's ancestors from whom they had derived their *in'ams*.[58] W.A.D. Inglis pointed out that many of the *kattubadis* had admitted indirectly in their depositions that all that class was engaged in a common cause.[59]

The second reason of their close connections was the caste factor. Not only Narasimha Reddy and many of the principal *kattubadis* but even many heads of the villages and principal *rayats* belonged to *Kapu* community.

It is, therefore, quite probable that Narasimha Reddy's relations, friends, the principal *kattubadis* and even *patels*, being alarmed at the threatened loss or curtailing of their *in'ams* and having consulted and complained to their leader, and at the same time the idea of bettering their lot, led them to an armed resistance against the English. Moreover, the people of the Ceded Districts in general and that of Cuddapah in particular, as indicated in the Inglis' report, had always felt confident that the settlement of landed tenures made nearly half a century ago, was to be permanent, and would not be altered in any way to their disadvantage. It was, therefore, to be expected that the serious changes attempted by the government would produce discontentment amongst the people in general.[60]

W.A.D. Inglis, Special Commissioner investigating the causes of resistance had attributed the remote cause of outbreak "to the frequent changes in the office of Collector in this District (Cuddapah)".[61] His observations about the people of and conditions in Cuddapah were absolutely correct. After all, he himself had been the acting Collector there for about six months, and as Special Commissioner he must have investigated all possible causes of resistance quite deeply.

The evidence shows that Narasimha Reddy had been preparing himself for a long drawn struggle against the English than a mere insurrection. It could be ascertained from the statements made before the magistrate by his close associates that he had in his possession a *sanad* (J.H. Cochrane thought it to have been a forged one) 'bearing the impression of a large seal in Persian Character' which he carried about with him stating that it had been sent to him by the Nawab of Golconda. The purport of the *sanad*, it was told, was an injunction to all the palegars in the Ceded Districts, who were formerly attached to the Nizam's territory, to assist him (Narasimha Reddy) in the object he had in view. With this *sanad* he also visited all the villages, which formerly comprised the *palaiyams* of his ancestors and obtained the goodwill and promised assistance. Initially he had the company of about 30 *kattubadis*, but gradually the number went on increasing, who all accompanied him from village to village. Narasimha Reddy confessed that he had shown the same *sanad* to the persons of influence in the Ceded Districts as well as in Hyderabad and not only obtained their support but also of others through them.[62] The prominent areas from where he could muster sufficient support were the palegars/ chiefs of Hyderabad, Kurnool, Owk, Banganapally and even Annegundy. These areas not only provided him with material support but could also easily use them as escape routes as well as hideouts—in case of emergency. However, the largest support that he got was from Koilkuntla, which incidently was his main centre of activities. His influence in Koilkuntla was so great that apart from the *kattubadis*, the people, including Brahmins, and the heads of the villages were at his back. It could not be denied that in this regard both the factors, the genuine support and fear, were working. In any case, it had made things so difficult for the English government, before and during the course of resistance, that it was almost impossible for them to get any correct intelligence about his activities and whereabouts.[63] Which *patel* or *kattubadi* was with the English or against them, was not easy to judge. Several letters written by J.H. Cochrane have given a detailed account of the events of the resistance.

It may be mentioned here that apart of his known associates in the campaign, Narasimha Reddy was duly assisted by the geographical conditions of the area. The government had got so much panicked that they could never make any correct assessment about the number of followers that the palegar had and their guess ranged from 200 to 9,000.[64] They even went to the extent of declaring an award of Rs. 1,000/- for the apprehension of Narasimha Reddy.[65] The task of the English had become all the more difficult and had become almost impossible for them to get any intelligence about the whereabouts, plans and activities of the palegar due to the active support that he was getting from the *patels*, *kattubadis*, *bhatta-vritti in'am* holders and the *rayats* in general.[66] It was only on 6 October 1846 that Narasimha Reddy could be captured.[67] After a trial lasting nearly 3 months, the Court of Faujdari Adalat delivered their judgment on 9 January 1847 and was hanged on 22 February 1847.

The resistance led by Narasimha Reddy and the report on its causes submitted by the Special Commissioner, W.A.D. Inglis (19 January 1847) had far reaching impact on the British policy towards the *in'am* lands. Both the things had forced the Court of Directors to give a second thought on the future course of action in regard to such grants, which 'have always been treated as hereditary.'[68] Howsoever, they might call this incident as 'insignificant in its political bearing'[69] or 'disaffection was local',[70] the very acceptance by the Court of Directors that the incident was 'connected with the course of treatment latterly pursued towards *in'ams*',[71] proves that their socio-economic policies lacked proper understanding of the priorities especially of the then conservative society. By simply quoting the 'insurrection of Narasimha Reddy', ascribed by the Court of Directors 'to a course of measures in violation at once of the stipulated and prescriptive rights of property in the district', as a cause of fresh 'discussion regarding the policy of disturbing long-existing rights of property in *in'am* lands',[72] gave added importance to that resistance.

The government issued a series of instructions upon which were founded the rules for the treatment of lapsed *in'ams*. The new rules declared that all *in'ams* held on grant at the date of the British assumption, and held by the same family at the time of the passing of Regulation XXXI of 1802, should be continued to the next heir on the same terms.[73] In those cases where the *in'am* had passed out of the original family, or had been fraudulently obtained or irregularly inherited; where it was claimed on invalid grounds, as through the female line, or by a collateral branch, in virtue of an illegal or suspicious adoption; or generally where there were any circumstances affecting the prior transmission of the *in'am* or the title of the existing claimant, the collector was required to report to the Board of Revenue and ultimately to the government. The immediate attachment of *in'ams* on the occurrences of lapses, which was a source of great distress, was prohibited.[74]

They accordingly announced certain principles, which were incorporated in the Minute of Sir Charles Trevelyan, the Governor of Madras (13 May 1859). The Governor in the same Minute also propounded certain rules on which the main Commission based its investigations. It was announced that if a land had for fifty years been in the possession of a person, or if those through whom he claimed, without the payment of land-tax, such length of possession should be held to be a good title to that land of *in'am*, whatever might have been the origin of the possession (whether held under any *sanad* or not).[75]

The *bhatta-vritti* and *khairatti in'ams* held respectively by the Brahmins and Muslims were enfranchised under the rules and were granted title-deeds. The *kattubadi in'ams*, irrespective of their origin, were also enfranchised, but the issue of title-deeds was suspended pending the completion of the new police arrangements. However, the whole extent of *in'am* lands was enfranchised on a quit-rent of five-eighths of the assessment. As regards the amount of quit-rent, it may be pointed out, as the study of the records preserved in the offices of the different Collectors/Deputy Commissioners shows that there were cases when the amount of quit-rent could be less than 5/8 and could be equal to the total survey assessment of the land.[76]

References

1. In this regard see for instance the palegars of Owk, Rayadrug, Harpanahalli, Chitvel, Nossam, Mullel, Kallibundah and different palegars of Gurramkonda district. *APSA, Cuddapah District Records (1802)*, 647/574; TNSA, *Madras Board of Revenue Proceedings*, 1 November 1802; *Col. Munro's Report Regarding the Ceded Districts* (1801-1802), ASO (D) Vol. 21 (67), Thomas Munro to the President and Members of the Board of Revenue dated 20 March 1802 (Hereafter, *Munro's Report Regarding the Poligars, 20 March, 1802*). ASO (D), Vol. 66, *Report of William Thackeray*, dated 8 September 1807. Dua, J.C., 'Poligars: Their rise in the Ceded Districts', *I.H.C.*, 1972, pp. 467-74. Sastri, K.N. Venkatasubba, *The Munro System of British Statesmanship in India* (Mysore, 1930), p. xiii.

2. Dua, J.C., *British Historiography: Eighteenth Century Punjab* (New Delhi, 1992), pp. 101, 108, 115.

3. TNSA, *Madras Board of Revenue Consultations*, 31 August 1801; *Col. Munro's Report Regarding the Poligars in the Ceded Districts with a Memorandum of Poligars, 1801-1802*, RSO (D), Vol. 66 (21), Letter from Thomas Munro to the President and Members of the Board Revenue, dated 12 August 1801. *Fifth Report*, pp. 88-89. *Munro's Report Regarding the Poligars*, 20 March 1802. Dua, J.C., 'Position of Patels and Karnams in the Ceded Districts during the first quarter of the nineteenth century', *I.H.C.*, Chandigarh, 1973.

4. APSA, *Cuddapah District Records* (1813), 655/246, Letter from Robert Ross, Collector to the Board of Revenue, 22 November 1813. *Report of the Madras Estates Land Act Committee* (Madras, 1938), 'Appendix', pp. 409-17. *Selections From the Records of the Madras Government*, New (Revenue) Series, No. 1, *A Collection of Papers Relating to the In'am Settlement in the Madras Presidency* (Madras, 1948), p. 347. Baden-Powell, B.H., *The Land-System of British India* (rpt. Delhi, 1974), 3 Vols., III, p. 82. Dua, J.C., 'Nature of the Poligar Revolts in the Ceded Districts During the First Half of the Nineteenth Century', *IHC* (Jadavpur) 1974, pp. 235-45.

5. *Munro's Report Regarding the Poligars*, 20 March 1802. Thomas Munro to the President and Members of the Board of Revenue, dated 12 August 1801, *op. cit.* TNSA, *Bellary Records* (1801), 396/453; *Selections From the Records of Bellary Districts-Political, Revenue and Agriculture Matters 1800-1857*, ASO (D), Vol. 73, Letter from Munro to William Patrie, President and Members of the Board Revenue, dated 22 June 1801. Francis, W., *Madras District Gazetteers: Anatapur* (Madras, 1905), p. 24.

6. *William Thackeray's Report*, dated 8 September 1807.

7. TNSA, *Bellary Records* (1801), 396/181, Letter from Munro to Wiliam Patrie, President and Members of the Board of Revenue, dated 30 July, 1801.

8. For further details about the widespread revolt of the palegars, see, TNSA, *Secret Despatches to England*, Vol. 2, pp. 66-70. Despatch of Edward Clive, 18 March 1801; *Secret Consultations*, Vol. 12, p. 118. Mornington to Edward Clive, 23 August 1800; *Military Despatches to England*, Vol. 31, pp. 136-37,

Despatch of Edward Clive, 15 October 1801; *Military Consultations*, Vol. 283, pp. 3554-58, Madras Council, 22 May 1801. *Fifth Report, op. cit.*, pp. 547-61. 'Report From Special Commission to the Governor in Council', Fort St. George, 5 April 1803. Rajayyan, K., *South Indian Rebellion: The First War of Independence 1800-1801* (Mysore, 1971), pp. 35-42, 123-213.

9. *Fifth Report, op. cit.*, pp. 614-41. 'Memoir of Mr. Hodgson, On Advantages of a Permanent Zamindari Settlement, 1806; pp. 547-61. 'Report from Special Commission to the Governor in Council, Fort St. George', 5 April 1803; pp. 317-35, 'Instructions issued to Collectors under the Presidency of Fort St. George, AS to Permanently Settling the Lands', 15 October 1799.
10. TNSA, *Madras Board of Revenue Consultations, 26 September 1805; Selections From the Old Records of Bellary District, 1800-1807*, ASO (D), Vol. 72, Thomas Munro to William Patrie, President and Members of the Board of Revenue, 25 August 1805. Dua, J.C., *Agrarian System*, p. 36. For a detailed discussion on the pre-British land ownership and rights of the *zamindars*, see, for example, Grover, B.R., 'Nature of Land-Rights in Mughal India', paper read at the Indian Economic History Seminar, Delhi, April 1961 and published in *Indian Economic and Social History Review*, Vol. I, 1963, pp. 1-23; 'Elements of Continuity and Change in Land Ownership and Rights from the Mughal Age to the Early British Administration in India', Presidential Address, Medieval India Section, *Indian History Congress*, 37th session, Calicut, 1976.
11. TNSA, *Madras Political Consultations/Proceedings*, 3 April 1801; *Selections ... 1800-1856*, ASO (D), Vol. 73, Munro to Josiah Webbe, Chief Secretary to Government of Fort St. George, 27 March 1801; *Papers regarding the Revenue Settlement 1801-1823*, ASO (D), Vol. 76, Letter from William Patrie etc. members to Edward Lord Clive, Governor in Council, 2 October 1801. *Munro's Report Regarding the Poligars*, 20 March, 1802. Also, Beaglehole, T.H., *Thomas Munro and the Development of Adminstrative Policy in Madras, 1792-1818, The Origin of 'The Munro System'*, Cambrige University Press, 1966. p. 62; Stein, Burton, *Peasant State and Society in Medieval South India*, New Delhi, OUP, 1980, p. 88, Chaudhuri, Shashi Bhusan, *Civil Disturbances During the British Rule in India, 1765-1857* (Calcutta, 1955), p. 129; Brackenbury, C.F., *Gazetteer of the Cuddapah District* (Madras, 1915), p. 48; Francis, W., *Gazetteer of the Bellary District* (Madras, 1904), pp. 46-40. It may be pointed out that in a few instances the rent was kept lower than the ordinary rents of the *sarkar* villages where the palegars produced the *sanads* of Lord Cornwallis and Sir Charles Oakley promising them reinstatement, or where raising it any further might have driven them into rebellion (Munro to Webbe, 27 March 1801).
12. They were: (i) those who were paid in money for their services, and were least numerous; (ii) those who were paid in land but were, notwithstanding farmers and regarded their service *in'ams* as a secondary object; and (iii) those who depended entirely upon their *in'am* lands for their subsistence and were more numerous than the first two categories.
13. *Munro's Report Regarding the Poligars*, 20 March 1802; also, Munro to Joshiah Webbe, Chief Secretary to Government of Fort St. George, 27 March 1801, *op. cit.*

14. *Ibid.*

15. Munro believed 'had they (the defaulters) met with any indulgence they would have continued to keep up the same number of peons next years, whereas by pressing rigidly the recovery of the defalcations, the more poor and timid will disband their followers—and the more powerful will feel themselves compelled to reduce the number of those which they retained'.

16. These palegars included four powerful ones, as mentioned earlier, that of Talpool, Vimlah, Chitvel and Nossam. The inferior ones included the palegars of Dasmuru, Ganjikota, Kalva, Kamalapuram, Kapotra, Mullel, Cumbun, Gurramkonda, Gudikota, Oopalur, Rarvah, Telpula, Tippreddipalle, Adoni, Baswapur, Bellary, Devankonda, Ghattu. Regarding the different types of the actions taken against the above palegars, see TNSA, *Bellary Records* (1801), 351/158; 396/106, 466, 374/92; 389/134; 376/137; 396/118; 396/480; 387/132; 396/463; 270; 396/4, 21, 26; 374/36, 39; 374/65; 66; 374/102, 103; 396/210, 472, 480; 351/158; (1800), 396/449; 452. APSA, *Cuddapah District Records* (1802), 647/572; 647/357; (1801), 647/560; (1802), 648/60; (1801), 647/551; 647/551; 647/59, 536.

17. TNSA, *Bellary Records*, (1802), 396/510, Order No. 275, 16 May 1802.

18. Letter from Thomas Munro to Lt. General Stuart, C-in-C. Madras, 11 November 1802, Gleig, *op. cit.*, I, pp. 335-39.

19. For Example, Harpanahalli was to have 2 Companies, Adoni 4 and Cumbum 3. TNSA, *Bellary Records* (1803), 404/236, Circular datd 21 May 1803 issued by Munro for the Collectors of Ceded Districts. Other things of note contained in the circular were:

(a) The salaries of the Sardar and Jamadar were fixed at Star Pagodas 6/- and 3/- respectively.

(b) Same writer could be appointed for upto 3 companies and would get salary from all.

(c) As there were no Jamadars before the regulations were passed, the collectors could nominate deserving Daffadars and fill up the Daffadars from Peons.

(d) Those who were disabled by wounds and the widows of every man killed on service were entitled to half the pay as pension.

(e) Contrary to the earlier practice, the peons were to desist from paying any *russom* to their Sardar.

20. Gribble, J.D.B., *A Manual of the District of Cuddapah* (Madras, 1875), pp. 104-07.

21. They were, for instance, the palegars of Chittoor, Dudikonda, Ghattu, Konakondla, Gudikota, Nileswaram, Punganuru, Hudgupa, Kullur etc., and also the attempts were foiled. See, TNSA, *Bellary Records* (1804), 375/132; 399/47, 101, 402/222, 381/170, 397/9, 398/232, 399/9; (1805), 315/190; (1806), 399/222, 364; (1804), 398/214, 222, 230, 399/26; (1806), 381/162, 410/176; (1802), 396/330, 650/8, 38; (1805), 632/146, 650/159, 225; (1806), 652/35; (1804), 650/71; (1805), 650/148.

22. Maclean, C.D., *Standing Information Regarding the Official Administration of the Madras Presidency in Each Department in Illustration of the Yearly Administration Reports* (Madras, 1879), 2nd edn., p. 90.
23. TNSA, *Revenue Despatch to Fort St. George,* 10 April 1804; APSA, *Cuddapah District Records* (1804), 633/48, Extract from a general letter from the Hon'ble Court of Directors, 10 April 1804.
24. TNSA, *Madras Board of Revenue Consultations/Proceedings,* 4 March, 1805; *Selections ... 1800-1856,* ASO (D), Vol. 73, Thomas Munro to the Board of Revenue, 22 February 805 (It was a very rare case that this letter was transmitted to Court of Directors without any comment by the Madras Government, TNSA, *Revenue Letter from Madras to England,* 8 March 1805, paras 178-79.
25. In this case a reference may be made to a 'Munro's Report of 1801'. He, for example, wrote: The economy of the Ceded Districts tracts became almost entirely depopulated. Hunnumuntgoond rated at 15,000 Cantaroy Pagodas in the Treaty Schedule produced Cantaroy Pagodas 4,000 only and Narsapoor rated at more than Cantaroy Pagodas 8,000 did not yield even 500 when they came under the Company'. See, TNSA, *Board's Consultations,* Vol. 296, p. 10592, Munro's Report, 20 August 1801.
26. APSA, *Cuddapah District Records* (1813), 640/26, Letter from Deputy Secretary, Fort St. George to the Collector of Cuddapah, 13 September 1813; Extract of a letter to the Chief Secretary to Government, 18 June 1813; Extract of a letter from the Secretary to Government in the Revenue Department, 10 September 1813; (1813), 640/39, Letter from P. Bruce, Magistrate, Zillah Court of Bellary to D. Hill, Secretary to Government, 6 September 1813, sent to the Collector of Cuddapah by D. Hill on 14 September 1813; (1813), 640/87. D. Hill to the Collector in Cuddapah, 28 September 1813.
27. APSA, *Cuddapah District Records* (1811), 637/183, Letter from W. Oliver, Secretary to the Collector in Cuddapah, 4 February 1811.
28. NAI, *Home Department—Land Revenue,* 17 May, 1845, Letter from Secretary, Board of Revenue, Fort St. George to Acting Chief Secretary to Government, 26 April 1830.
29. *Ibid.*
30. NAI, *Home Department—Land Revenue,* 24 April 1847 (4-9), Letter from Sir Montgomery Bart, Offg. Secretary to Government of Fort St. George, 10 March 1847; Letter from G.A. Bushley, Secretary to the Government of India to Montgomery, 24 April 1847.
31. NAI, *Home Department—Land Revenue,* 19 August, 1843 (4-10), Letter from J.D. Bourdillon, Secretary, Board of Revenue to Arbuthnot, Acting Principal Collector Cuddapah, 30 June 1843.
32. NAI, *Home Department—Land Revenue,* 19 August, 1843 (4-10), Letter to J.H. Thomas, Secretary to Government, Fort St. George, 19 August 1843.
33. *Madras District Gazetteers, Bellary District,* Vol. II (Madras, 1930), p. 63.

34. Carpenter, Mary, *Last Days of Raja Ram Mohun Roy in England* (Calcutta, 1915), p. 113. Roy, Raja Rammohan, *Exposition of the Practical Operation of the Judicial and Revenue Systems of India* (London, 1832), pp. 69-77.

35. For the application of these Regulations/Acts See, 'Report by Mr. W.T. Blair on the entire operations of the In'am Commission', 30 October 1869, *Selections from the Records of the Madras Government New* (Revenue) *Series No. 1, A Collection of Papers relating to the In'am Settlement in the Madras Presidency* (Madras 1948), pp. 311-326. (Hereafter, *the In'am Settlement Papers*). For details about the Regulations see, *The Regulations of the Government of Fort St. George in Madras, 1801-34.*

36. Frykenberg, Robert Eric, 'The Silent Settlement in South India, 1793-1853: An analysis of the Role of Inams in the Rise of the Indian Imperial System', in Frykenberg, Robert Eric (ed.), *Land Tenure and Peasant in South Asia* (New Delhi, 1984), pp. 37-53, p. 39. Krishnaswami, S.Y., *Rural Problems in Madras: Monograph* (Madras, 1947), p. 58. Apart from the known ways of giving land grants, a recent research/book has given new dimensions to the subject. It has come to light that "Early medieval India also witnessed a parallel custom of putting the actual sale of landed property in the form of a sacred donation. Sometimes the sale of property was openly recorded and donation was proclaimed as the purpose of the sale. In such cases the vendor is the state and the donor is the individual who has purchased the land and requested the government to make it a rent-free holding. But sometimes the king himself is the donor and yet he happens to have actually sold out the property to the person on whose request the grant had been made. Without reading between the lines it is not possible to detect the real character of these characters which have been intentionally given the patent look of a land grant." The author has quoted such cases from Rajasthan, Uttar Pradesh, Bihar, Bengal, Gujarat, Madhya Pradesh, Maharashtra, Goa, Orissa, Andhra Pradesh, Karnataka and Tamil Nadu. Om Prakash, *Early Indian Land Grants and State Economy* (Allahabad, 1988), pp. 85-182.

37. *The In'am Settlement Papers,* pp. 342-54. Moreover, the *In'am Fair Registers* preserved in the collectorates (I have personally checked these registers in the Anantapur Collectorate) give a detailed description of the number, character, value, and nature of *in'ans* in every village of that district.

38. *The Inam Settlement Papers,* p. 311. 'Report by Mr. W.T. Blair on the entire operations of the *In'am* Commissioner', 30 October 1869, p. 211. TNSA, *Papers Regarding the Revenue Settlement 1801-1823,* ASO (D), Vol. 76, Thomas Munto to the Board of Revenue, 1 July 1801. *Correspondence between the Collector, the B/Rev. and the Government regarding the Settlement of Fuslies 1230 and 1245 (1820-1835).* ASO (D), Vol. 78, Letter from the Secretary to Government to the Board of Revenue, 12 July 1825.

39. See for example, Grover, B.R., 'Elements of Continuity and Change in the Land Ownership and Rights from the Mughal Age to the Early British Administration in India', Presidential Address, Medieval India Section, *Indian History Congress* (Calicut, 1976).

40. 'Report of Mr. W.T. Blair....', 30 October 1969, *op. cit.*, p. 312.

41. *Ibid.*, Also, APSA, *Cuddapah District Records* (1808), 635/48, Letter from Secretary Fort St. George to the Collector of Cuddapah, 21 March 1800.

42. TNSA, *Bellary Records*, 384/54; and *Selecttions from the Old Records of the Bellary District, 1800-1807*, ASO, Vol. 72, Circular issuedby Thomas Munro, 14 April 1807. J.C. Dua, 'Positions of the Patels and Karunums ...', *op. cit.*

43. TNSA, *Revenue Department, Minute of Consultation*, No. 533, 26 April 1845. Also *Ibid.*, pp. 312-313. A letter from Home Department (Revenue) to the Secretary to Government Fort St. George (22 August 1846) reveals that some *in'amdars* produced *sanads* even 150 years old granting them the *in'ams*, Collector of Cuddapah advocated to the Board of Revenue for the continuation of the *in'ams*; and the Government did not have any objection to that. See, NAI, *Home Land Revenue* (22 August 1846), pp. 11-15, 'Cuddapah', instructions re. Certain *in'ams* in'.

44. TNSA, *Official Report of a Revolt by Polegar Narasimha Reddy in Koilcuntla Taluk in 1846*, ASO (D), Vol. 113 (Vol. III), Letter from S. Scott, Agent to the Governor to the Chief Secretary to Government, Fort St. George, 11 May 1847. *Selection of Papers relating to the Revolt of the Poligar Narasimha Reddi of Koilkuntla* (1846), ASO (D), vol. III, (Vol. I), Letter from J.K. Cochrane, Ag. Magistrate to H.C. Montgomery, Offg. Secretary to Government, 15 April 1847. (Hereafter, *Official Report of a Revolt*, Vol. III and *Papers Relating to Revolt*, Vol. I respectively).

45. TNSA, Col. *Munro's Correspondence regarding the Survey and Ryotwari Settlement of the Ceded Districts, 1802-1827*, ASO (D), Vol. 79, Munro to his subordinate collectors regarding the modes of conducting the Ryotwari Settlement, 30 Settlement 1802.

46. TNSA, *Mintues of Consultation*, Judicial, 9 October 1846.

47. *Ibid.*, Also *Official Report of a Revolt by PalegarNarasimha Reddy in Koilkuntla Taluk in 1846*, (ASO (D), Vol. 112 (Vol. II), (hereafter *Official Report of a Revolt*, Vol. II), Letter ın W.A.D. Inglis, Special Commissioner at Cuddapah to Sir H.C. Montgomery Bart Offg. Secretary to Government, Judicial Department, 19 Januray 1847.

48. *Ibid.*

49. TNSA, *Selections from the Old Records of the Bellary District,1800-1807*, ASO (S), Vol. 72, Letter from Thomas Munro to the Chief Secretary to Government, 30 September 1801, Also, *Thomas Munro's Report Regarding the Poligars*, 20 March 1802.

50. TNSA, *Selection from the Old Records of the Bellary District, 1800-1807*, ASO (D), Vol. 72, Thomas Munro to the Secretary of Police, 10 April 1806.

51. APSA, *Cuddapah District Recrods* (f. 1231), 419/348, Letter from D. Hill, Secretary to Government to the President and Members of the Board of Revenue, 18 September 1821. Also quoted in the letter from W.A.D. Inglis, 19 January 1847, *op. cit.*

52. In this regard, see the observations made in Dua, J.C., 'Comparative Position of the Village Headmen During the Early British Rule in the Punjab and the Madras Presidency', *Punjab History Conference,* Patiala, 23rd session, 1987. Also in, Dua, J.C, *Agrarian System, op. cit.,* p. 124.

53. Letter from W.A.D. Inglis, 19 January 1847, *op. cit.*

54. *Ibid.,* It is quite strange that there is some discrepancy in the reports submitted by W.A.D. Inglis and J.H. Cochrane. As against the information regarding *Kattubadi in'ams* provided by Inglis, according to Cochrane the position was: There were a total number of 8985 *kattubadis* in the Cuddapah District. According to the latest regulatoins each *kattubadi* would get an *in'am* of worth survey assessment Rs. 23-10-0, for one life and thereafter was to be remunerated in cash. The implications of the Regulation was that *in'ams* of 1557 *kattubadis* were to be resumed on the occurrences of lapses. The *in'ams* of 1396 *kattubadis* which were in excess of the amount fixed were proposed to be reduced on their demise to the required standard (and were to be for one life only). The emoluments of remaining 6032 *kattubadis* were to be raised to the minimum standards. (Letter of J.H. Cochrane, 11 September 1847, *op. cit.*).

55. TNSA, *Proceedings of the Board of Revenue,* 10 August, 1848; *Minutes of Consultation,* Judicial, 27 May 1847, 4 Januray 1848 and 8 February 1848. *Papers relating to Revolt,* Vol. I, Letter from J.H. Cochrane, Ag. Magistrate to H.C. Montgomery, Offg. Secretary to Government, 15 April 1847, (Letter from W.A.D. Inglis, 19 January 1847, *op. cit.,* NAI, *Home, Land Revenue,* 17 May 1845 (10-12), Letter from Secretary, Board of Revenue, Fort St. George to Acting Chief Secretary to Government, 26 April 1830.

56. Letter from W.A.D. Inglis, 19 January 1847, *op. cit.*

57. Letter from W.A.D. Inglis, 19 January 1847, *op. cit.*

58. Letter from W.A.D. Inglis, 15 September 1847, *op. cit.*

59. Letter from W.A.D. Inglis, 19 January 1847, *op. cit.*

60. *Ibid.*

61. *Ibid.*

62. Letter from Cochrane, J.H., 15 September 1847, *op. cit., Papers Relating to Revolt,* Vol. I. Letter from Cochrane, J.H., Acting Collector to the Secretary to Government (Judicial Department), 12 July 1846. Two things could be learnt from these letters: (1) the important persons he met including Panpa Khan of Kurnool, Latchman Royadu, palegar of Jutapolur and Rama Krishna Reddy, palegar of Wunpurty, both in Hyderabad and Palegar of Owk, and (2) he asked the Owk palegar to request Pumpaputy Raju, Palegar of Annaugundy to write to other palegars in the Bellary district.

63. In this regard see, for example, *Papers Relating to Revolt,* Vol. I, Letter from Cochrane, J.H., to the Secretary to Government, 10 August 1846; 7 September 1846, 16 November 1846.

64. Cochrane, J.H., in his letters to the Officer Commanding, Ceded Districts, 11 July 1846, and to the Agent to the Governor, 12 July 1846 (*Official Report of a*

Revolt, Vol. IV), and to the Secretary to Government (Judicial Department), 12 July 1846 (*Papers Relating to Revolt,* Vol.) put the figures at 9000. Cochrane in his letter to the Magistrate of Guntur, 20 July 1846 (*Offcial Report of a Revolt,* Vol. IV) put the figures at 3,000. But in his letter to H.C. Montgomery, Offg. Secretary to Government, 15 Aprl 1847 (*Papers Relating to Revolt,* Vol. I) stated that the number of followers never increased more than 200. Commander Detachment 19th Regiment in his letter to the Officer Commanding Field Detachment 19th Regiment, 29 July 1846 (*Official Report of a Revolt,* Vol. III) put the figures at 4,000.

65. *Papers Relating to Revolt,* Vol. I, Cochrane to the Secretary to Government, 10 August 1846. TNSA, *Minutes of Consultation, Judicial Department,* No. 441, 27 July 1846.
66. See for example, *Official Report of a Revolt,* Vol. IV, Cochrane, J.H., to the Agent to the Governor at Kurnool, 25 July 1846. *Papers Relating to Revolt,* Vol. I, Cochrane to the Secretary to Government, 28 July 1846 and 10 August 1846.
67. *Papers Relating to Revolt,* Vol. , Letter from Cochrane to the Secretary to Government, 7 October 1846.
68. TNSA, *Revenue Despatch to the Honourable Court of Directors,* 2 November 1846, No. 49.
69. Report of Blair, W.T., 30 October 1869, *op. cit.*
70. *Official Report Regarding the Revolt,* Vol. V, Extracts Minutes of Consultations, 2 March 1847.
71. TNSA, *Judicial Despatch from the Court of Directors,* 13 October 1847, No. 19.
72. *Ibid.*
73. The instructions issued were through—*Minutes of Consultation,* 9 May 1848; *Minutes of Consultation,* 11 May 1848; *Proceedings of the Board of Revenue,* 19 June 1848; *Minutes of Consultation,* 4 July 1848 and *Board's Circular Order,* 27 July 1848. For details see, *The In'am Settlement Papers,* G.O. No. 677, Revenue, 22 March 1861, pp. 183-93; G.O. No. 2330, Revenue, 7 December 1860, pp. 193-202; and Report by W.T. Blair, *op. cit.*
74. *Ibid.*
75. Quoted in the Report of W.T. Blair, *op. cit.*, pp. 314-15.
76. The study of, for instance, the *In'am Fair Registers* in the Collector Office, Anantapur shows that one Duar Chola Terimungala Rao Maharah, Paddinonikalva Village, Rayachoti Taluk was confirmed an *in'am* on 1/8th quit rent but in 1935 he was fully assessed. There are cases where ½ and in some ¼ quit-rent was charged. Then there were *in'ams* which were confirmed only for one-two lives. Amongst various other registers, one known as *Statement showing the Village Service In'ams Fully Assessed in the Taluk of—in the District of*—itself means that the *in'amdars* incorporated in that were not holding *in'ams* on concessional rates. While in *Quit Rent Register of Personal In'ams in the Taluk of—in the District of*—to quote one example, Kadavella Devappa, who had acres 46.58 in dry and 17.01 in wet land and whose survey assessment was Rs. 89-14-9, was paying same amount as quit-rent.

Lecture III

Comparative Study of the Nature of the Two Phases of Palegars Resistance

The palegar resistance, though apparently looks like a challenge to the English system of law, revenue, production and property relations and thus offers the most intelligible clue to proper understanding and a rational evolution to its nature, could easily be bracketed together with the spontaneous resistance against the English East India Company which continued in India for nearly hundred years preceding the revolt of 1857. A close examination of the history of India as a whole shows that this process had started right since the early eighteenth century, the period which witnessed the emergence of rebel *zamindars* of different categories and the palegars. Their main aim was to seek greater share in the power over, and thus in the revenues of, their region. These revolts were sometimes directed against the state, and sometimes against the nobles in the respective regions who, with the emerging political situation had begun to dictate state actions. However, during the course of the period, the scuffle between different *zamindars*/palegars was also not uncommon. In certain areas, including the ones under study, the *zamindars* acted as 'local despots', and were in an uncompromising conflict with the state authorities. They allied with the state rulers only due to two broad reasons, (i) in the face of the fear, and (ii) with an objective of promoting and protecting their self-interests *vis-a-vis* the others within the region. Whenever they found themselves strong enough, they would be up in arms. However, as their interests were invariably narrow and parochial, they could not effectively incorporate the interests of other fellow *zamindars*/palegars. They relied mainly on the support from peasants, smaller *zamindars* and the local officials, but that support was forthcoming again because of fear or for promoting individual interests. In these conditions of unfattered political and military adventurism, it is noteworthy that none of the adventurer *zamindars*/palegars was either strong enough to be able to win the allegiance of others or in a position to replace the state power.

They would struggle separately for their individual fortunes and thereby threatened each other's position and achievements. In the event of success in the establishment of dominance by some over the others, the former would, however, definitely seek to institutionalize validation of their spoils which necessitated the need of a centre to legitimize their acquisitions.[1]

The second half of the eighteenth century witnessed the beginning of the process of the British Conquest of India and the consolidation of the English rule was accompanied by serious discontent and resentment among the people. The popular discontent took the form of armed resistance led, amongst others, by the palegars of the Ceded Districts.[2] Since the military contingents were maintained by the palegars out of the revenues assigned to them, the tendency on the part of the state was to set the revenue demand at the highest rate possible so as to secure the greatest military strength for the state and to keep as little as possible with the palegar so that his military and political designs were kept in check. Whereas the palegar would try to collect the maximum, legally or even otherwise, to enhance his social and military status and to keep his political hopes alive. As such, the main point of conflict between the state and the palegars was the size of latters share in the revenues. The dilemma faced by the palegars was that it was difficult for them to collect the revenues, pay that or *peshkash* or both to the authorities without harming their own interests. The geographical conditions of the Ceded Districts had also contributed to make the situations there still worse. It is well known that usually, the areas, which were protected in some measures by ravines or forests or hills, were more likely to defy the authorities than those in the open plains. During the Mughal period these areas were known as *mawâs* and *zor-talab,* as opposed to the revenue paying villages, called *ra'iyati.* Refusal to pay the revenue or *peshkash* or both, as the case might be, on the part of the palegars, and attempts, on the part of the Company, to force them not only to pay the same but also curb their military and political power, led the former to show resistance. It frequently turned into armed conflict and became an important feature of the political situation of the time.[3]

The Company aimed at the liquidation of the landed elite and favoured corporate village groups or the individual *rayat* rather than the palegars, making them (the *rayats*) responsible to Government for revenue. Barrington Moore, Jr., for example, writes, "A paternal attitude toward the peasantry, a romantic and self-serving notion that the strong and simple folk could and should be the source and justification of their power, constituted a powerful theme in British policy throughout the occupation, even if peasant benefit therefrom are dubious.[4] It can, as such, be safely argued that the palegar resistance was part of the, to use the term used by Kathleen Gough, 'Restorative Movements'. It was either against the conquest itself and the imposition of heavy revenue or *peshkash* on the palegars, or retaliatory attempts to drive out the British after they had dispossessed a palegar or a raja for failing to pay the revenues/*peshkash* and had replaced him with some other claimant to the *palaiyam* or with direct company's administration. Their aim was, to quote Kathleen Gough again, "complete annihilation or expulsion of the British and reversion to the previous government and agrarian relations".[5]

The nature of the palegar resistance during the early nineteenth century has been dealt in great detail by Professor K. Rajayyan.[6] Though concentrating mainly on the areas other than the ones presently under discussion, general remarks on the palegar institution and the resistance have been discussed in great length. An analysis of the above painstaking work shows that if the British were at one extreme and called the palegars as 'robbers, freebooters, marauders and the like', Professor Rajayyan is on the other extreme, calling the palegar resistance as 'The First War of Independence' and 'the most widespread of all the liberation wars of the pre-Congress epoch and the first and the last violent popular struggle of any formidable dimensions in the annals of British India.' However, as has been discussed earlier, the palegars were subjected to, at least at the time of the inception of this institution, set and well defined rules, duties and responsibilities. It may or may not be true about the earlier period, but it is quite evident from the contemporary records of Haider and Tipu that during 'the last decades of the eighteenth century' a new phenomenon could be traced in the working of the palegar institution.

The Company took severe action against the palegars when the *peshkash*, fixed and demanded, was refused. That is notwithstanding the fact that palegars were up in arms immediately after the districts were ceded to the Company. Technically speaking the English were following the policy already adopted earlier by Haider Ali and Tipu Sultan as far as the fixation of the land revenue and the amount of *peshkash* were concerned. That is a different matter that they (palegars) could evade complete extinction or annihilation earlier either due to the then political situations or by using the tactic of yielding allegiance to each new master and had not only managed to reassert their authority but had appeared even stronger.

It is true that large sections of peasants and artisans as well as locally recruited 'peons' joined the palegar resistance and formed its backbone. It, however, does not mean that they had whole-hearted sympathy for the palegars. They had joined it because of their own grievances and hardships.[7] In the Ceded Districts where the *rayatwari* system of land revenue 'predominated the peasant holding land on the rights of the *rayat*' was equally exploitative as was the case in its counterpart in the *zamindari* regions, where big landed proprietorship predominated. As a matter of fact, the essential distinctions between the various types of revenue systems introduced by the East India Company and the forms of agrarian relations accruing out of them did not alter the basic fact that the agrarian system and methods of exploiting the peasants developed in one and the same direction throughout the country. The land revenue policy of the British authorities pursued the aim of obtaining highest possible revenues and maintaining them at the achieved level. Under earlier regimes the revenue demand was usually adjusted according to the results of the harvest. Furthermore, the peasant could cultivate more or less land in keeping with the availability of family labour and other things. These elements of flexibility had disappeared under the English rule. As such, it can safely be presumed that the peasants were not blind loyalists.[8]

As regards those who formed the militia of the palegars, their loyalty to the latter was as doubtful as that of the palegars themselves towards their suzerain. If the palegars were more interested in the advancement of the power of their own *palaiyams*, their military personnels were more concerned about their own service *in'ams*, known as *kattubadi in'ams*. When they were offered employment and the grant of fresh *sanads* in the name of the Company, especially when the palegars were officially relieved from all military services their loyalty towards the palegars became extremely shaky. Once they were convinced that there was no intention of resuming their *in'ams*, and thinking that it was much more likely that the palegars would be driven out, they considered their own tenure under the Company more sure than under the palegars.[9]

The institution of caste also does not seem to have helped in making the palegar resistance as a popular movement. This institution, of course, provided a way of organizing the local community in such a way as to make the state authority something superfluous rather than something to be changed when things went wrong. As a matter of fact, it was practically from the beginning of the twentieth century when 'The imperial system had...created a new political arena within which to compete for rights, precedence, and resources in the public domain', that the caste political associations 'became a recognized institutional means for voicing demands in the media and in the urban context of government decision making'.[10]

It, as such, can be maintained that the partisans of the theories like the 'national awakening', or 'The First War of Independence' in regard to the palegar resistance have relied more on present sentiment than on contemporary evidence. The reader may judge their case as presented in their own writings. Our main concern is with what late eighteenth and the early nineteenth century sources/ authorities have to say, It will be seen that they, at any rate, put the greatest store by the political, economic and administrative causes of the resistance and know little of national consciousness.

Right since the disintegration of the Vijayanagar empire, except when they were forced especially by the rulers like Haider Ali and Tipu Sultan, the palegars had followed the practice of the evasion of the payment of taxes/revenue/*peshkash*. They had once again got a free hand when the areas came under the Nizam. All this had not only resulted into the increase of their territorial possessions but had also enhanced their economic and military power. It, however, goes without saying that they were landed *zamindars*, having set economic and military duties to perform for which they had been assigned lands. It was obligatory on their part to pay the revenues or *peshkash* or both, as the case might be. Their practically continuous success in evading to perform their obligations was tantamounted of their independence.

So long as there was more than one centre of political power the palegars continued to have divided loyalties. When one area was transferred from Vijayanagar to the Golconda or Bijapur or the Mughals, the Marathas and so on, the palegars of that area were slow to transfer their loyalties to their new masters. Similar was the situation when the areas came under the East India Company. The palegars often supported their deposed or earlier chief, either because of their loyalties or for their self interests, against the Company as long as there was the slightest hope of his restorations.[11] Gribble has rightly pointed that the palegars had 'seen so many successive governments that it can be understood they did not expect the British rule would be a permanent one'.

If the palegar resistance in the Ceded Districts is not judged in isolation and if an attempt is made to draw parallels with other such incidents, especially the events of 1857, the question of non-acknowledgement of the English suzerainty on the part of the palegars may also appear as one of the important factors of their resistance.

The British occupation in India was looked upon as nothing short of the usurpation of the authority by them. They could in no way be less 'usurper' than was Haider Ali or for that matter palegars were considered by them. The source of the establishment of English control over the Ceded Districts was either in sword or the political intrigues that Nizam was unable to understand. There may not be any evidence to prove it but hypothetically it could be observed that it might be a matter of non-recognition of the English as the suzerain power by the palegars, which led the latter to resist the English authority. In any case, whether usurper or legitimate, the restrictions imposed by the Company's government upon the palegars were bound to invite resistance from them.

It may, thus, be observed that this phase of the palegar resistance was based on the traditional links and qualified loyalties between the peasants and the palegars or the petty chieftains. This resistance was wholly local and isolated in character lacking required mass appeal. Its main objective was the restoration of the political, administrative and economic powers lately or heretofore enjoyed by the palegars. It was, like other contemporary, 'Restorative revolts', backward looking and in no way attracted any modern feeling of nationalism. Nor did it have any 'modern understanding of the nature and character of colonialism or the building of a new society on the basis of new social relationships.' The palegar resistance was represented by a leadership, which was, like the nature of opposition offered, pure and simple, traditional in character. The leaders were also absolutely ignorant about the changing world around them. Despite the fact that the English power had to, at times, deploy large armies to suppress the resistance, the palegars could not pose a real challenge to the Company. However, the palegars could not be denied the credit of the great contribution made by them in a long history of resistance against the foreign rule. Their resistance as well as other such revolts in India laid the foundations of valuable local traditions of struggle against the British rule.[12]

Phase II

"A strict observance of our treaties," spoke Benjamin Disraeli in the House of Commons on 27 July 1857, "the rigid maintenance of laws and customs of the people, and, above all, a faithful respect for our guarantees of their land...these were the sources of our strength, and upon these our great Indian statesmen always insisted. But, Sir, of late years a new principle appears to have been adopted in the Government of India...Everything in India has been changed. Laws and manners, customs and usages, political organizations, the tenure of property...everything in India has either been changed, or there is a suspicion among the population that a desire for change exists on the part of our Government".[13] In brief, for Disraeli, the primary mistake of British rule in India was its increasing tendency to interfere with the established rules and customs. It is true that the above observations were made while tracing the causes of the revolt of 1857, but they as well hold good for the resistance of 1846-47. Narasimha Reddi's resistance had taken place just about a decade before the revolt of a great magnitude like that of 1857. It was the first against the English policy towards the *in'am* lands at least in south India. In this regard, they completely neglected the value of the indigenous institutions as a means of giving social happiness and material well-being to the people.[14] They paid no attention, or, it seems, tried to test the then universal belief that the Indians generally did not care who ruled them as long they were left free to follow their immemorial customs. The result was that along with the other disgruntled elements, like the palegars, the English had also aroused the hostility of conservative elements generally by their seeming intention to subvert the traditional social order.

The first instructions pertaining to the *in'am* lands issued by Thomas Munro, were that all *in'ams* which had been granted under the *sanad* of Haider Ali, or Tipu Sultan, or some of the more ancient princes or their ministers were not to be resumed.[15] In case of the areas under Cuddapah Collectorate, Munro directed Alexander Stodart, the Collector, that 'the *in'ams*, though granted originally by Amildars or inferior revenue officers may be continued', provided that they had been held since the extinction of the Nawab's power and commencement of Haider's Government, without interruption. His interpretation about such *in'ams* being that such long possession constituted 'a kind of prescriptive right'.[16]

It is important to note that a considerable number of old *in'ams*, which had been suppressed due to various reasons by the different *karnams* of Ceded Districts were also restored.[17] As a matter of fact, Munro was neither in favour of the resumption of the *in'ams* nor wanted that they should be replaced by cash salary or pension. According to him, a pension could never be considered as a compensation for the loss of landed property. "It is neither so honourable nor so secure," he argued. He also reasoned, "The amount of their Enam lands in the Ceded Districts is so inconsiderable that Government might, with hardly any perceptible loss of revenue, continue them as they are, until they should gradually revert by the failure of the different families by which they are at present enjoyed".[18] It would not be wrong to conclude that his land settlement as well as *in'am* policy laid the true foundation of peace in the turmoil stricken Ceded Districts. In addition to the reasons mentioned above, he continued *in'ams* on the ground that it was as 'difficult for the *In'amdar* to verify his title as for the Sirkar to disprove it,'[19] and permitted the holding of service lands by village officials (like *patels, karnams* etc.) upto 10 percent of their village revenue, with a view to facilitate the rapid creation of private property in land.[20] He did not resume any of the lands of religious and charitable institutions, but, however, exercised control against misappropriation.[21]

As regards the *kattubadi in'ams*, Thomas Munro in 1801 observed that the loss to the revenue by the continuation of those *in'ams*, 'would not be so great as it may at first sight appear'.[22] As late as 1841, A. Mellor, Collector of Bellary, while commenting 'on the propriety of making a direct payment in money...in lieu of assignments of land sanctioned' in *kattubadi* tenure, pointed out that those *in'ams* had been 'considered from time immemorial, (though in fact service *in'ams*), as a kind of *meeras*, little differing from simple hereditary property'. He warned, "To disturb this arrangement would produce a feeling of insecurity and discontent among the whole body of *in'amdars*".[23] Quoting Chaplin's views on the same subject with approval Mellar further explained that since they were accustomed to the possession of *in'am* land, and to transmit that possession from father to son, 'they naturally feel strong attachment to their hereditary property and would not willingly relinquish it for any pay, however, high'. By giving detailed figures, though about Bellary district, he tried to stress that *in'ams* were more economical than paying *kattubadis* cash salaries.

The correspondence pertaining to the year 1843 shows that even in that year *in'ams* in the Ceded Districts were 'confirmed and continued in perpetuity' on the recommendation of the Collector, the Board of Revenue, the Governor of Fort St. George and authorization by the Governor General.[24]

Right since the formation of the Ceded Districts in 1800, there had been a continuous desire and demand on the part of the English administrators to conduct a survey and inquiry into the nature and extent of the *in'am* lands. The inquiry conducted by Thomas Munro in the initial stages was described by the authorities in the Madras Presidency as 'superficial' and inadequate.

It could not ascertain the extent of 'Sirkar land surreptitiously held as Enam'. Stating that they had 'long wished that an enquiry should be instituted respecting them (*in'ams*)', the Board of Revenue asked William Chaplin (1809) to 'institute a general enquiry into Enam Lands, or at all events threat to do so'.[25] The Board of Revenue through their Minute (9 May 1811) simply asserted that the Government had a right to dispossess the *in'amdars* if they renounced their service upon which they held their lands.[26] Chaplin, in the same year reiterated that though the *in'ams*, under the rules, were 'resumable at the pleasure of the ruling authority', and 'however strictly the scrutiny into them may be carried on', the object could 'hardly be accomplished without instituting new rules for investigating the validity of titles'.[27]

By the above discussion, an attempt has been made to stress upon the fact that if the Government had reason to believe that many of the *in'ams* were held upon forged documents, it was no more than their duty, and perfectly consonant to justice, to investigate such cases, and resume the lands proved to be so held. In any case, they should have borne in mind that the investigations and decisions were ought to be speedy, final, and good. Had there been a proper provision for that purpose, there would have been little to complain of. Even in 1842, as is evident from Lord Elphinstone's Minute of the same year, the position of investigation was no better than what it was in 1801.

The inordinate delay on the part of the English Government in conducting a proper investigation into the *in'am* lands, and even grant of fresh *in'ams*, despite periodic orders for an enquiry, had given hopes to *in'amdars* about the continuation of their land grants in perpetuity. In India every situation held for a long while has a tendency to become hereditary (e.g. *patel*, *karnam*, *qazi*, *in'amdar* etc.) and the natives of all classes are peculiary ready in advancing claims".[28]

History and common sense alike show that an armed resistance or a rebellion can never take place without provocation. The question is, had the English Government given such provocation? The palegar Narasimha Reddi along with some of his breathren and the *bhatta-vritti* and *kattubadi in'amdars* saw their power, their privileges, and their perquisites crumbling away from them, and they tried to gird themselves up to arrest the devastation.

The conversion of hereditary pensions/*in'ams* into personal annuities was, to quote Disraeli, "confiscation by a new means, but on most extensive, startling and shocking scale".[29] The palegars were reduced to utmost humiliation and almost to absolute beggary. The government had practically disturbed the settlement of property by their conduct with regard to the resumption of *in'ams*, by abolishing the principle of heredity, and by changing the *in'ams* into annuities.

It was the responsibility of the government to protect the society and the social order, and, as far as possible, 'every member of the society from the injustice or oppression of every other member of it', and 'establishing an exact administration of justice'.[30] Before promulgating a legislative enactment, the government should have, through local enquiry and research, looked into the traditions of the society.[31] "Whether the state should interfere at all; on what principle; with what limitations; what property, if any, should be . . . inalienable; what means of protection, temporary or permanent, the state should create or allow to be created; are all questions to which", remarked Mr. Justice West, "clear answers, appropriate to the people and their circumstances, should be obtained by a Government anxious to deal beneficiently and consistently with the problems connected with the occupancy of the soil in this country".[32]

Thomas Munro was quite critical of the activities of the civil and military officers who by acting precipitately, often upon wrong information, involved government in hostilities.[31] He not only blamed their misconduct for the insurrection of petty chiefs, but also cautioned his government "not to be led away by fanciful theories founded on European models, which will inevitably end in disappointment".[34]

The opinion expressed by Thomas Munro was in no way less than a warning to the future English administrators also that nothing disgusted the natives of this country more than the resumption of traditionally revenue free lands, and their resumption would set the whole people against the English. Though initially only *bhatt-vritti* and *kattubadi in'ams* were being resumed or their nature was being changed, it could rightly be contemplated that the other category of *in'ams*, as was indicated by different Regulations, could no longer be safe either. Apart from the brahmins and the *kattubadis*, the *patels, karnams* and even weavers, carpenters, smiths, barbers, washermen, potters or for that matter every artisan and labour were primarily paid by an allotment of *in'am* land. Their *in'ams* were 'adequate to keep a family in comfort as tropical needs go, though not in luxury'.[35] In case of any danger to their *in'ams*, the resentment was obvious. The English government could hardly expect tenderness from those, whose *in'ams* had been resumed, or their hereditary nature scrapped, or those whose *in'ams* could be adversely affected in the foreseeable future.

The tradition of the *in'am* lands had been so deep-rooted in the Indian social order that not only in the Ceded Districts but in other parts of India also, when the subject of their resumption came, it became a topic of lengthy discussions, difference of opinions amongst the English administrators, and even led to the cases before the Privy Council. In Punjab (1849-53), for example, there was difference of opinion between the two Lawrences, Henry and John, whether the grants assigned for the services no longer wanted, or could not be maintained, were to be continued. Whereas Henry held that 'grants ought to be continued, although the obligation of service might be remitted,' John wanted that 'these grants must at once be curtailed, and provision made for their cessation on the demise of present incumbents.'[36]

The case of Khurda (Orissa), which was incidentally also under the *rayatwari* system, was not only interesting but also almost similar to that of the Ceded Districts. Khurda also witnessed resistance (1838 onwards) due to the resumption and assessment of certain revenue-free tenures. The agitation spread from a small and influential class to the whole estate. H.A.D. Phillips, criticising the English policy, pointed out, 'To say the least, it is an unwise policy to interfere with customary rights.' The ruling given by the Privy Council in this regard, as stated by Phillips, pointed out:

> The distinction between the grant of an estate burdened with certain service, and the grant of an office, the performance of whose duties are remunerated by the use of certain lands, and have ruled that a tenure of the former description cannot be resumed merely on the ground that

the service is no longer required . . The *Sanad* did not state that the tenure was to cease, if the services ceased. The Privy Council held that the grant had been made *proservitiis impensis et imendendis*—partly as a reward for past, part an inducement for future services. . they may be liable to forfeit the tenure if they willfully fail in the performance of . . duty, are not liable to have their land resumed, because there is no longer any occasion for the performance of . . particular service.[37]

The case of *bhatta-vritti* and *kattubadi in'ams* in the Ceded Districts was in no way different to that of the *in'ams* in Khurda. Despite suggestions, warnings and cautions, the Company initiated the policy of the resumption of the *in'am* lands. The hereditary palegars backed by a proud ancestry, and the *in'amdars*, with a long possession of lands for generations, had undoubtedly momentous consequence in the continuous continuation of the mainstream of life, and so alike in a political and social view the extinction of these classes was fraught with serious repercussions. Lord Macaulay aptly remarked in 1844 that "of all forms of tyranny the worst is that of a nation over a nation."[38]

As far as Narasimha Reddy was concerned, undoubtedly, he had his own reasons of discontentment. He was the successor of one of those chiefs who had already, willingly or unwillingly, submitted to the English. The submission of a particular chief or a palegar of a *palaiyam* did not necessarily guarantee the loyalty and fidelity of his successors. The terms accepted by a palegar might not be acceptable to his successor, and the paramount power had to win over the loyalty of the new palegar afresh, which might not be so easily forthcoming. Moreover, the prerogative exercised by the paramount power in matters of succession to a *palaiyam* and the right to recognize or de-recognize a palegar greatly helped in sowing the seeds of resistance, especially in case of Narasimha Reddy. He took full advantage of the situations created by the English policy towards the *in'am* lands and found a favorable opportunity to give vent to his own grievances. However, in any case the resistance was not for getting freedom but to force the government to take corrective measures.

The noteworthy aspect of this resistance was the co-operation of the general people, the *kattubadis*, brahmins, some of the fellow palegars, the country people and the villagers of the different social status including the *patels*. The brahmins, who had become hostile to the English because of the latters' policy towards the *bhatta-vritti in'ams*, used their influence in the society and created better atmosphere for the resistance. It helped, to a great extent, in keeping the British intelligence at bay and people would never give correct report about the whereabouts of Narasimha Reddy and his associates. E.J. Hobsbawn has classified the resistance of Narasinha Reddy and his followers as 'social banditry.'[39] Wherever such activities called forth the support of large bodies of common people, as distinct from personal retainers or mercenaries, wherever some initiative in the struggle passed to inhabitants of the affected area, one cannot in fairness deny the existence of a resistance movement.[40]

This shows that this phase of resistance was not aimed to gain any political power, as was the case with the palegar resistance of late 18th and early 19th centuries, but was essentially a socio-economic one in which a considerable section of the people felt, however dimly, the stirring of a common impulse.

References

1. Dua, J.C., *British Historiography: Eighteenth Century Punjab* (New Delhi, 1992), 'Preface' and 'Introduction'. Dua, J.C., 'Review Article' on K. Rajayyan, *South Indian Rebellion: The First War of Independence 1800-1801* (Mysore, 1971), in *The Indian Historical Review*, Vol. II, No. 2, January 1976, pp. 490-92. (Hereafter, 'Review Article'). Alam, Muzaffar, *The Crisis of Empire in Mughal North India: Awadh and the Punjab, 1707-48* (Delhi, 1986), pp. 13-17.
2. The armed resistance was in a large proportion led by Hindu and Muslim petty rulers, former revenue agents under the Mughals, tribal chiefs in hill regions, *zamindars* and the palegars. The most important leaders and the regions of the resistance were Raja Chait Singh and other Hindu and Muslim *zamindars* of Awadh in 1778-81; the subsequent revolt of Vizier Ali, the deposed Nawab of Awadh, in Banaras, Gorakhpur and surrounding areas in 1799, the resistance of the palegars and their peasants in Tinnevelly, North Arcot, and the Ceded Districts in 1800-05; the uprising of the Chuar tribesmen of Midnapore in 1799; the revolt of the Pazhassi Raja of Malabar in 1796-1805; and almost immediately afterwards, an insurrection further south in Travancore and Cochin by Velu Thampi. For further details in this regard see, Chaudhuri, S.B., *Civil Rebellion During the British Rule in India (1765-1857)*, (Calcutta, 1955), pp. 56-58, 74-76 and 125-32. Ghosh, Benoy, 'Prepolitical Rebellions in Bengal', *Frontier*, Calcutta, Vol. V, Nos. 27-29, 14 October 1972, pp. 9-14. Gough, Kathleen, 'Indian Peasant Uprisings', *Economic and Political Weekly*, Vol. IX, Nos. 32-34, Special Number, August 1974, pp. 1391-1412, also in Desai, A.R. (ed.), *Peasant Struggles in India* (Delhi, 1982), pp. 85-126. Chandra, Bipin, Tripathi, Amalesh, De Barun, *Freedom Struggle* (New Delhi, 1980), pp. 41-42, Dua, J.C., 'Review Article', *op. cit.*
3. For the geographical conditions of the Ceded Districts, see for example, TNSA. *Extract from Mr. William Thackeray's Report, 8 September 1807*, ASO (D), Vol. 66. Hamilton, Walter, *A Geographical, Statistical and Historical Description of Hindustan and the Adjacent Countries* (London, 1820, reprint, Madras 1990), II, pp. 323-27. For similarities of political situations during pre-British period see, Habib, Irfan, *The Agrarian System of Mughal India (1556-1707)*, (Bombay, 1963), pp. 318-51.
4. Moore, Jr. Barrington, *Social Origins of Dictatorship and Democracy: Lord and Peasant in the Making of the Modern World* (Penguin Books, 1969), pp. 348-49. Also see, Baden-Powell, B.H., *The Land-Systems of British India* (Oxford, 1892, reprint Delhi, 1974), II, pp. 20-21. Komarov, Erik, 'Content and Principal Forms of the Evolution of Agrarian Relations in India in the 19th Century', *New India Studies by Soviet Scholars—"Social Sciences Today"*, No. 33, 1976, pp. 34-47.
5. Gough, Kathleen, *op. cit.*
6. Rajayyan, K., *South Indian Rebellion: The First War of Independence 1800-1801* (Mysore, 1971).
7. Dua, J.C., 'Review Article', *op. cit.*

8. Dua, J.C., *Agrarian System in South India: Some Aspects* (New Delhi, 1990), p. 54. Komarov, Erik, *op. cit.* Rothermund, Dietmar, *The IndianEconomy Under British Rule and Other Essays* (New Delhi, 1983), pp. 4, 31. *East India Sugar: an Enquiry* (London, 1824), p. 8. 'The Land Revenue in Madras', *The Calcutta Review*, 1852, No. 34, p. 322.
9. TNSA, *Bellary Records* (1801), 391/34, Letter from George Garrow to Thomas Munro, 8 December 1801. *Col. Munro's Report Regarding the Poligars in the Ceded Districts with a Memorandum of Poligars (1801-1802)*, RSO (D), Vol. 62 (21), Letters from Thomas Munro to the President and Members of the Board of Revenue, 12 August 1801. *Selections from the Old Records of the Bellary District 1800-1807*, ASO (D), Vol. 72, Letter from Thomas Munro to the Secretary of the Committee of Police, 10 April 1806.
10. Ludden, David, *op. cit.*, pp. 195-96.
11. For such type of Parallels during the Mughal period see, Khan, Ahsan Raza, *Chieftains in the Mughal Empire During the Reign of Akbar* (Simla, 1977), pp. 219-20.
12. Dua, J.C., 'Review Article', *op. cit.*, 'Nature of the Palegar Revolts in the Ceded Districts During the First Half of the Nineteenth Century: A Case Study', *Indian History Congress Proceedings* (Jadavpur, 1974), pp. 235-45. Gough, Kathleen, *op. cit.*, Bipan Chandra, Amales Tripathi and Barun De, *op. cit.*
13. *Parliamentary Debates*, 3rd Series, Vol. 147, 27 July 1857, pp. 440-472; Speech by Benjamin Disraeli, excerpts given in the form of an article, 'Military mutiny or National Revolt', in Embree, Ainslie T. (ed.) *India in 1857: The Revolt Against Foreign Rule* (Reprint Delhi, 1987), pp. 9-21, especially 10-11.
14. Chaudhuri, S.B., *Civil Disturbances During the British Rule in India 1765-1857* (Calcutta, 1955), p. 207.
15. TNSA, *Selections From the Old Records of the Bellary District 1800-1807*, ASO (D), Vol. 72, 'Instructions issued by Col. Munro, Principal Collector to Mr. Cochrane, Collector of Bellary, 31 December 1800.
16. *Ibid.*, 'Instructions for Alexander Stodart'.
17. Thomas Munro to Board of Revenue, 13 May 1805, *op. cit.* Regarding the various reasons and circumstances under which the *karnams* used to suppress the information, also see, Dua, J.C., 'Position of the Patels and Karnams in the Ceded Districts during the First Quarter of the Nineteenth Century', in Bhattacharya, Sabyasachi (ed.), *Essays in Modern Economic History* (New Delhi, 1987), pp. 23-40.
18. Letter from Munro to the Board of Revenue, 13 May 1805, *op. cit.*
19. TNSA, *Selections from the Records of Bellary District—Political, Revenue and Agriculture Matters*, ASO (D), Vol. 73, Letter from William Chaplin to the Board of Revenue, 24 April 1814. Also, Sastri, K.N. Venkatasubba, *The Munro System of British Statesmanship in India* (Mysore, 1930), p. XIV.
20. *Ibid., Selections...*, ASO (D), Vol. 72, Thomas Munro to the Board of Revenue, 23 June 1801.

21. TNSA, *Revenue Despatch of the Court of Directors,* 30 August 1809, para 169.
22. TNSA, *Col. Munro's Report Regarding the Poligars in the Ceded Districts with a Memorandum of Poligars 1801-1802,* RSO (D), Vol. 62 (21), Letter from Thomas Munro to the Board of Revenue, 12 August 1801.
23. TNSA, *Correspondence regarding the Grants of Land Instead of Money Allowance to the Police Establishments and the Revision of Assessment 1841-1850,* ASO (D), Vol. 28 (75), Letter from A. Mellor, Collector Bellary to the Secretary and Board of Revenue, 13 March 1841.
24. NAI, *Home Department Land Revenue,* 7 October, 1843, 9-14 (b) Letter from A. Mellor, Collector of Bellary to C. Lovell, Acting Secretary to the Board of Revenue, Fort St. George, 10 May 1843; Same to same, 25 July 1843; Home Department, Revenue to the Chief Secretary to the Government, Fort St. George, 7 October 1843 (dispatched on 13 October 1843).
25. For the difficulties faced by the collector in making the settlement, see, TNSA, *Bellary Records* (F. 1219), 417/348, Letter from Chaplin, Collector to the Board of Revenue, 2 November 1809'; and for the remedy suggested see 417/462, Letter from Secretary, Fort St. George to the collector of Bellary, 13 November 1809.
26. TNSA, *The Proceedings of the Board of Revenue on the Introduction of Village Lease in the Ceded Districts—1811,* ASO (D), Vol. 31 and 32, Minute of the Board, 9 May 1811.
27. APSA, *Cuddapah Records* (1811), 637/352, Letter from William Chaplin to the Board of Revenue, 10 June 1811.
28. TNSA, *Minutes of Consultations,* 9 October 1846, para. 8.
29. Speech by Benjamin Disraeli, *op. cit.*
30. 'Adam Smith on government responsibility', in *Readings in Economic and Social History,* Selected and Edited by M.W. Flin (London, First Edition 1964, Reprint 1965), p. 178-79.
31. Kurnool Collectorate Library, *Papers Relating to Reform of Police in India,* 1861, J/154, Minute by the Hon. Mr. Fullerton, 27 April 1816.
32. Kurnool Collectorate Library, *Selection from Papers on Indebtedness and Land Transfer,* J/276, Mr. Justice West's "The Land and the Law in India", 1872.
33. Thomas Munro to the R. Hon, C.B. Bathurst, 28 September 1821, Gleig, II, pp. 50-60.
34. Thomas Munro's Minute, 31 December 1824, *op. cit.*
35. Venkataramani, K.S., *The Indian Village: A Ten Year Plan* (Svetaranya Ashrama, Mylapore, Madras, 1936), pp. 6-7.
36. Temple, Sir Richard, *Lord Lawrence* (Macmillan, 1936), pp. 61-62.
37. Phillips, H.A.D., *Our Administration of India* (London, 1886), pp. 31-33.
38. Cited in Rao, M. Ramachandra, *The Development of Indian Polity* (Madras 1917), p. 61.

39. Hobsbawn, E.J., 'Social Bandits: Reply (to Blok)', in *Comparative Studies in Society and History*, Vol. 14, No. 4, September 1972, p. 504.
40. For this type of opinion, also see, Chaudhuri, S.B., *op. cit.*, p. 261.

Select Bibliography

This study is primarily based on original source material, inscriptions, travelogues, and memoirs etc. available in manuscript, printed or published forms. Different category of source material has been mentioned under a separate head along with the place where it was consulted.

I am obliged to Professor B.R Grover (Delhi) and Mr. Ziauddin Ahmed (Hyderabad); Dr. T.R. Vasantha Rao (Madras); and Dr. PM. Rathnam (Madras) for helping me in translating/deciphering Persian, Tamil and Telugu sources respectively.

1. Manuscript Sources

A. Tamil Nadu State Archives, Madras

Bellary District Records (Handbook to the Revenue Records of the Ceded Districts (Madras, 1932), which is both chronological and subject-wise, has been extremely helpful in the study of these records.)

Government of Madras, Revenue Department, 6.0. No. 2108, 21 August 1907.

Judicial Despatches From England, Vols. 1-22. Judicial Despatch to England, Vols. 1-30.

Madras Board of Revenue Consultations (1790-1*30), also known as Proceedings of the Board of Revenue.

Madras Political Consultations/Proceedings, Vols. 1-43.

Madras Revenue Consultations (1792-1*30).

Madras Secret Consultations/Proceedings, Vols. 1-48.

Military Consultations, Vols. 71-346.

Military Despatches to England, Vols. 15-108.

Minutes of Consultations, Judicial, Vols. 1-676.

Military Sunthy Books, Vol. 61(1784).

Public Department: Sundries (Public Sundries). These volumes contain records/minutes etc. in Munro's own handwriting, 1801-1806.

Revenue Department, Minutes of Consultation, Vols. 10-843.

Revenue Despatches From England, 1792-1830.

Revenue Despatches to England, 1792-1830.

Secret Despatches to England, Vols. 1-6.

B. Andhra Pradesh State Archives, Hyderabad

Asafia Documents (Persian), esp. pertaining to Tipu Sultan's period.

Hukam-Nama-i-Tipu Sultan (Persian).

Cuddapah District Records. (These records were formerly in Madras and later on transferred to Hyderabad. Some of these documents were consulted at Madras Archives and rest in Hyderabad. For these documents also the Handbook mentioned earlier was very useful.)

C. National Archives of India, New Delhi

The relevant portions of the following series:

Foreign Department Secret Consultations

Foreign Political Sescret Proceedings.

Foreign (Secret) Proceedings of Secret Select Committee, 4 January to 20 July 1768.

Fort St. George Records (1799). Home Department Revenue Records. Hyderabad Residency Papers.

Records of Government of India in the Imperial Record Department, 1748-1859, Political Branch, 1789-1859.

Survey of India Memoirs.

D. Karnataka Secretariat, Bangalore

Mysore Records (in Carton Boxes), Box No. 28. Contains the English correspondence.

E. Collector Office, Anantpur

Inam Fair Registers.

Statements Showing the Village Service Inams.

Quit Registers of Personal Inanis.

F. Tehsildar Office, Cuddapah

Pension Registers.

2. Printed Primary Sources:

Officially Printed/Published

A. Tamil Nadu State Archives, Madras

Aitchison, C.U., A Collection of Treaties, Engagements and Sanads Relating to India and Neighbouring Countries, 9 Vols. (Calcutta: Government Press, 1909).

Baramahal Records (1792-1799).

Bundla Ramasawamy Naidoo, Memoir on the Internal Revenue System of Madras, 1820 (Madras, 1908), II, M.R.O. Vol. 259.

Col. Munro's Correspondence Regarding the Survey and Ryotwari Settlement of the Ceded Districts, 1802-1827, ASO(D), Vol. 79.

Col. Munro Report Regarding the Poligars in the Ceded Districts with a Memorandum of Poligars, 1801-1802, ASO(D), Vol. 62(21).

Collector's Report on the Economic Condition of the District (Bellary), 1885, Vol. (336) 61.

Collector 's Report on the Revision of Assessment, 1859, ASO(D), Vol. 71.

Correspondence Between the Collector, the Board of Revenue and the Government Regarding the Settlement of Fuslies, 1230-1245 (1820-1835), ASO(D), Vol. 78.

Correspondence Regarding the Grants of Lands Instead of Money Allowance to the Police Establishments and the Revision of Assessment 1841-1 850, ASO(D), Vol. (28)75.

Extract From Mr. William Thackeray 's Report, 8 September 1807, ASO(D), Vol. 66.

Graeme, H.S., Report on the Polyams of Chittoor (Madras, 1893).

General Reports of the Board of Revenue to the Hon. the Governor in Council, Sent Home to the Hon. the Court of Directors (General Report. of the Board of Revenue), Vols. 10-20.

Indian Record Series - Vestiges of Old Madras 1640-1800 Traced from the East India Company's Records, Vol II

Lushington, S.R., Report Regarding the Tinnevelly Polegars and Sequestered Poliams (1800, Reprint 1916)

Official Correspondence Between the District Magistrate Cuddapah and the Government of Madras Regarding the Riot Committed by the Mussalmans of Cuddapah Town Which Ended in Death of Mr Macdonala IC S, Sub-Collector and Joint Magistrate - 1832-1833, ASO(D), Vol 109

Official Report of a Revolt by Poligar Narasimha Reddy in Koilkuntla Taluk in 1846, ASO(D), Vols. 112, 113, 114 and 115.

Papers Connected with the Reorganisation of the Police in the Madras Presidency (Madras, 1869).

Papers on Poligar Peshcush (Madras, 1808).

Papers Regarding Revenue S 1801-1 823, ASO(D), Vol. 76

Papers Relating to Pohgar War (Tmnevelli, 1916)

Proceedings of the Board of Revenue, 'Settlement', 'Mr Place's Report on the Jaghire', 6 October 1795

Records of Fort St George Diary and Consultation Books (Madras Records Office, 1910-43).

Report the Madras Estates Land Act Committee (Madras, 1938)

Selection of Papers Relating to the Revolt of the Poligar Narasimha Reddi of Koilkuntla (1846), ASO(D), Vol. 111.

Selection of Papers From the East India House Relating to the Revenue, Police, and Civil and Criminal Justice 'Under the Company's Government in India (4 Vols.),'Vol. Ill, ASO(B), 74A.

Selections From the Old Records of the Bellary District, 1800-1807, ASO(D), Vol. 72.

Selections From the Records of the Bellary District - Political, Revenue and Agricultural Matters, 1800-1856, ASO(D), Vol. 73.

Selection From the Records of the Madras Government, New (Revenue) Series, No 1, A Collection of Papers Relating to the main Settlement in the Madras Presidency (Madras, 1948).

Statement of Police Committee on the Administration of District Police in the Madras Presidency (Madras, 1902)

The Annual Register for the Year 1783 (2nd Ed London, 1800)

The Fifth Report of the Select Committee on the Affairs of the East India Company. Madras Presidency, Vol. II (London, 1812, Madras, 1883)

The Proceedings of the Board of Revenue on the Introduction of Village Lease in the Ceded Districts - 1811, ASO(D), Vol. 31 and 32.

The Regulations of the Government of Fort St George in Madras, 1801-1834.

B. Andhra Pradesh State Archives, Hyderabad

Confidential Note on the Ceded Districts, Hyderabad, Memorandum (Begumpet, Deccan, 18 January 1932).

East India (Constitutional Reforms), Report of the Indian Stales Enquiry Cpommittee ('Financial,) 1932, Presented by the Secretary of State for India to Parliament by Command of His Majesty, July 1932 (Sinila Government of India Press, 1932).

Khan, Yusuf Husain (ed.), Farmans and Sanads of the Deccan Sultans (Hyderabad: Andhra Pradesh State Archives, 1963).

Law Department: The Andhra Pradesh Code (in five volumes), Vol. V, Regulations and Acts in Force in the whole of the Andhra Pradesh, 1822-1862 (Director, Government Press, Hyderabad, 1963).

Supplementary Report of the Special Committee Appointed to Investigate Certain Facts Relevant to the Economic and Financial Relations Between British India and Indian States (Ceded Area), 1932 (New Delhi : Government of India Press, 1932).

C. Maharashtra State Archives, Bombay

Forrest, G.W., Selections From the State Papers Preserved in the Bombay Secretariat, Maratha Series, Vol. 1(1885).

Poona Residency Correspondence (Vol. III, No. 63 and 121).

Ray, N.B. (c The Allies War with Tipu Sultan (Vol. III of the Poona Residency Correspondence, 1937).

Selections From the Records of the Bombay Government, No. 4, Report on the 'Village Communities of the Deccan', by R.N. Goodine, 10 October 1845.

D. Cuddapah Collectorate, Cuddapab

Selections From the Records of the District of Cuddapah No. 1 (Cuddapah: Collectorate Press, 1870).

E. National Library, Calcutta

East India Company, Debates at the East India House in the General Court of the Proprietors of East India Stock, 8 Vols. (London, 18 13-14), Vol. II.

East India: Sugar - An Enquiry (London,. 1824).

Parliamentary Debates From the Year 1803 . . . forming a Continuation of the Work entitled 'The Parliamentary History of England from the Earliest period to the year 1803' - Published Under the Superintendence of TC Hansard, 22 November 1803 - 28 February 1820, 41 Vols. London. Relevant Debates Relating to India.

The Intercepted Correspondence Etc. as published by the French Government From the Originals Taken on Board etc. trans. (London, 1804).

'The Land Revenue in Madras', The Calcutta Review, No. 34, 1852.

F. Karnataka Secretariat, Bangalore

Madras Administration Report, 1921-22, Part II.

Mysore State Papers. Selections, Vol. II (Mysore, 1922).

Selections From the Records of the Mysore Commissioner's Office (Bangalore, 1864).

G. Kurnool Collectorate, Kurnool

Papers Relating to Reform of Police in India, 1801, J/ 154. Selection of papers .on indebtedness and Land Transfer, J/276.

3. Printed Primary Sources: Published Privately

Arbuthnot, Sir Alexander J., Major General Sir Thomas Munro, Bart., Governor of Madras. Selections of His Minutes and Other Official Writings, 2 Vols. (London, 1881).

Beatson, Lieutenant-Colonel Alexander, A View of the Origin and. Conduct of the War with Tippoo Sultan; Comprising a Narrative of the Operations of the Army Under the Command of Lieutenant-General George Harris and the Seige of Seringapatam (London, 1800).

Bayley, W.H., and Hudleston, W., Papers on Mirasi Right: Selected From the Records of the Madras Government (Madras, 1862).

Ellis, F W., Papers on Mirasi Right; Selected From the Records of Government and published by Permission. Compiled by W.H. Bayley of the Madras Board of Revenue (Madras, 1862).

____,Replies to Seventeen Questions Proposed by the Madras Government of Fort St. George Relative to Mirasi Right with Two Appendices (Madras, 181*).

_____,Three Treatises on Mirasi Right by Francis W. Ellis, Lt. Colonel Blackburn, Sir Thomas Munro. Ed. by C.P. Brown, Madras Civil Semce (Madras, 1852).

Gleig, G.R., The Life of Major General Sir Thomas Munro, Bart. and KC.B. Late Governor of Madras, 3 Vols. (Lon don, 1830).

Gopal, M.H., British Sources of the Economic, Political and Social History of Mysore State, 2 Vols.., i, 1799-1812, Purnaiah 's Administration, ii, 1813-1832, Raja '5 Adminis tration, Bombay, 1993.

Kausar, Kabir, Secret Correspondence of lipu Sultan (New Delhi, 1980).

Mahalingam, T.V. (ed.), Mackenzie Manuscripts: Summaries of the Historical Manuscripts in the Mackenzie Collection, 2 Vols. (Madras University, Vol. I, 1972; Vol. 11, 1976).

Martin, R. Montgomery (ad.), The Despatches, Minutes and Correspondence of Marquis Wallesley KG. During his Ad ministration of India (2nd edition, London, 1840), Vol. 1V.

Owen, Sidney J. (ad.), A Selection From the Despatches, Trea ties, and other Papers of Marquess Wellesley, During his Government of India (Oxford, 1877).

_____,A Selection From the Despatches... Relating to India of the Duke of Wellington (Oxford, 1880).

Parliamentary Debates, 32d series, Vol. 147, 27 July 1857, pp. 440-72; Speech by Benjamin Disraeli, excerpts given in the form of an article, 'Military Mutiny or National Revolt', in Embree, Ainslie T. (ad.), India in 1857: The Revolt Against Foreign Rule (Delhi, 1987), pp. 9-21.

Rao, P. Hari, The Madras Acts (Criminal: 1802-1 929) Containing All the Local Enactments Relating to Criminal Law with Legislative Changes and Case-Law Brought Upto-date (Madras, 1930).

Ross, Charles (ed.), Correspondence of Marquess Cornwallis, 3 Vols. (2nd Edo. London, 1859).

Sajunlal. K., 'A Few Unpublished Letters of Sir Thomas Munro', in k7dian Historical Records Commission Proceedings, Vol. XXXI, Pait2, 1955.

Sastri, K.N. Venkatasuba, 'More Light on Sir Thomas Munro'. in Indian Historical Records Commission Proceedings, Vol. XIV, 1937.

_______, The Munro System of British Statesmanship in India (Mysore: University of Mysore, 1930).

Tour, M.M. D La, The History of Hyder Shan alias Hyder Ali Khan Bahadur, and his son Tipu Sultan, revised and corrected by His Highness- Prince Gholam Mohammed (Delhi, 1976).

4. Oriental Manuscript Library, Madras

Taylor, William, A Catalogue of Oriental Manuscripts in the Library of (Late) College, Fort St. George, 3 Vols. (Madras, 1857-1862).

List of Mackenzie Inscriptions In the Ceded Districts (Madras, 1935).

Oriental Historical Manuscripts in Tamil Language, Translated with Annotations, 2 Vols. (Madras, 1862, 1935).

5. Office of the Director of Archaeology, Mysore

Haider Nama, by a Hindu Officer in Haider All's Service (Mss. 1784).:

Elay Joze Correa Peixotio, Memoirs of Hyder Ally From the Year 1758-1770 (Mss. 1170)

6. Persian Texts (In English Translation)

Crisp, B., The Mysorean Regulations, Translated from the Persian (Calcutta, 1792).

Elliot, H.M., and Dowson, J., History of India as Told by its Own Historians, 8 Vols. (London, 1866-1877), Vol. IV.

Kirkpatrick, William (tr. and ed), Select Letters of Tippoo Sultan to Various Public Functionaries Including his Principal Military Commanders - Governors of Ports and Provinces, D and Commercial Agents etc. (London: Black, Pam' and Kingsbury, 1811).

Mirza Iqbal, Ahwal-i-Haider Nayak. Supplement to N/s Haidar, tr. and ed. Col. W. Miles (London, 1864).

Tarikh-i-Faristah by Muhammad Qasim Hindu Shah, Farishtah, and Tarikh-i- Sultan Muhammad Quth Shahi English translations in Briggs, John, History of the Rise of the Mohammedan Power India, 4 Vols. (Calcutta, 1910). In Vols. II and UI respectively.

7. Inscriptions

Annual Report of Epigraphy (South India) for the years 1887-194415 (Madras, 1887—1955). Report for the years 1912 and 1914.

Epigraph/a Carnaica, Vol.11 (Bangalore. 1898; Revised Mysore, 1973).

Iyer, KR. Srinivasa (tr.), Inscriptions in the Pudukkottai State, Part I and 11(1941,46), Part II.

Narasimhachai, R. (ed.), Archaeological Survey of Mysore, Annual Report: 1912, Vol. IV, A Study by S. Setter, Editor (Karnatak University, Dharwar, 1977).

Report of the Mysore Archaeological Survey, 1924

Sewell, Robert, Archaeological Survey of South India: List of the Antiquarian Remains in the Presidency of Madras, com piled under the Orders of Government, 2 Vols. (Madras, 1882-84) Vol. I

The Historical Inscriptions of South India, Collected Till 1923, ed. by S. Krishnaswanu Aiyangar (Madras, 1932).

8. Survey, Travel, Memoir

Buchanan, Francis Hamilton, A Journey From Madras Through the Countries of Mysore, Canara and Malabar /800-180/, 3 Vols. (London, 1807; 2nd edn. Madras 1870).

Dames, Longworth (tr. with notes etc.), An Account of the Countries Bordering on the Indian Ocean and Their Inhabit ants Written by Durate Barbosa and Completed About 1518, 2 Vols. (London, 1918), Vol. I.

Dubois, Abbe, Hindu Manners, Customs and Ceremonies, Trans. from French and edited with notes by Henry K. Beauchamp (London, 1924).

Heyne, Benjamin, Tracts, Historical and Statistical, on India; With Journals of Sevens! Tours Through Various Parts of the Peninsula. Also An Account of Sumatra, in a Series of Letters (London, 1814).

Lockman, John, Travels of the Jesuits, Being translations from the Letters edifiantes etc. curieuses, ecrites des Missions etrangers, par les Missionaires de la compagnie de Jesus (20 March 1792), 2 Vols. I. Reproduced in Aiyar, R. Sathyanatha, History of the Nayaks of Madura (Oxford University Press, 1924), pp. 296-323.

Narrative of Domingos Paes (written probably, A.D. 1520-22); Chronicle of Fernao Nuniz (written p A.D.1535-37). Both reproduced in Sewell; Robert, A' Forgotten Empire: Vijayanagar: A Contribution to History of India (New Delhi: Publication Division, .1962), pp.228-78 and 279-376 respectively.

Stillivan, John Sr., Tracts Upon India; Written In the years 1779, 1780 and 1788 with Subsequent 'Observations (Lon don, 1795).

9. Census

Das, B.K. , Census of India, Series 9 Karnataka. District Census Handbook, Bellary District, Part X - A and B, Village and Town Directory (Government of India, 1986).

______,Census of India 1981, Series 9 Karnataka, Part X-A, Town Directory (Government of India, 1987).

Lindsay, A.W.C., Report on Mysore General Census of 1871 (Bangalore, 1874).

Rao, S.S. Jaya, Census of India 1981, Series 2, Andhra Pradesh, Part XII, Census Atlas (Government of India, 1988).

Rice, Benjamin Lewis, Report on the Mysore Census of 1881 (Bangalore, 1884).

Shekhar, A. Chander, Census 1961 (A.P.): District Census Handbook Cuddapah District (1961).

Stuart, H.A, India, Census Commissioner, Census of India, 1891, Vol. XIII: Madras Report (Madras: Government Press, 1893).

10. Manuals and Gazetteers

Brackenbury; C.F., Madras District Gazetteer - Cuddapah (Madras, 1915).

Chetty, M. Gopala Krishna, A Manual of the Kurnool District (Madras, 1886).

Francis, W., Madras District Gazetteers, Anantapur (Madras, 1905).

____Bellary (Madras, 1904).

Gribble, J.D.B., A Manual of the District of Cuddapah in the Presidency of Madras(Madras, 1875).

Hunter, W.W., The Imperial Gazetteer of India, Vol. 1. (London, 1885).

Imperial Gazetteer of India: Provincial Series: Madras, 2 Vols. (Calcutta, 1908).

Kelsall, J., Manual of the Bellary District (Madras, 1872).

Maclean, C.D., Manual of (/j Administration of the Madras Presidency in illustration of the Records of the Government and the Yearly Administration Reports, 3 Vols. (Madras, 1885-1893).

____ Standing information Regarding the Official Administration of the Madras Presidency in Each Department in Illustration of the Yearly Administration Reports (Madras, 1877;2nd edn. 1879).

Madras District Gazetteer, Bellary Division, Vol. II (Madras, 1930).

Pate, H.R., Madras District Gazeiteer: Tinnevelly (Madras, 1917).

Pharoah & Cot A Gazetteer of Southern India with the Tensserim Provinces and Singapore, 2 Vols. (Madras, 1855).

Rao, C. Hayavadana, Mysore Gizetteer, Vol. IV, Administration (Bangalore, '1929).

Stuart, J.A.;A Manual of the Tinnevelly District (Madras, 1879).

Sturrock, J., Madras District Manuals, South Canara (Madras, 1894).

Thorton, Edward, The Gazetteer of the Territories Under the Government of East India Company and the Native States of the Continent of India, Vol. III (London, 1854).

11. Dictionary and Glossary

Brown,. C.P. Telugu-English Dictionary (1854 edition).

Tam Lexican, 6 Vols. (Madras: Madras Law Journal Press, 1934).

Yule, Henry, and Burnell, A.C., Hobson-Jobson: A Glossary of Colloquial Anglo-Indian Words and Phrases and of Kindred Terms, Etymological Historical, Geógr4hical and Discursive, Ed. by William Crooke (London, 1903; Reprint Delhi, 1968).

Wilson, H.H., A Glossary of Judicial and Revenue Terms and of Useful Words Occurring in Official Documents Relating to the Administration of the Government of British India from.

....Languages (London, 1855, 2nd edn. Delhi, 1968).

Sircar, D.C., Indian Epigraphical Glossary (Delhi, 1966).

12. Official Histories

Malcolm, John, The Political History of India From 1784 to 1823, 2 Vols. (London, 1826).

Mill, James, The History of British India. Ed. with notes and continuation by Horace Hayman Wilson, Vol. VI (London, 1840 and 1858). Both the editions have been used in the present work.

Wilks, Lieut. Colonel Mark, Historical Sketches of the South India' in an Attempt to Trace the History of Mysore . . . .(1810). Edited with notes by Murray Hammick, 2 Vols. (Mysore, 1st Vol. in 1930 and 2nd in 1932).

13. Modern Works

Aiyangar, S. Krishnaswaini, Evolution of Hindu Administrative institutions in South India (Madras: University of Madras, 1931).

Aiyar, R. Sathyanatha, History of the Nayaks of Madura. Ed. with Introduction and Notes by S. Krishnaswami Alyangar (Oxford University Press, 1924).

Alam, Muzaffar, The Crisis of Empire in Mughal North India: Awadh and the Punjab, 170 7-48 (Delhi: OUP, 1986).

Ali, B. Sheik, English Relations with Haider All (Mysore University, 1963). .

_____History: Its Theory and Method. 2nd edn. (Madras: Macmillan, 1981).

Ali, M. Athar, The Mughal Nobility Under Aurangzeb (Aligarh,1966).

Appadorai, A., Economic Conditions in South India, 2 Vols. (Madras, 1936).

Baden-Powell, B.H., The Land Systems of British India, 3 Vols. (Oxford, 1892; Reprint Delhi, 1974).

Baliga, B.S., Studies in Madras Administration, 2 Vols. Madras: India Press, 1960).

Balihatchet, Kenneth, Social Policy and Social Change in Western India, 1817-1830 (London, 1957).

Barber, William, J., British Economic Thought and India, 1600-1858, A Study in the History of Development Economics (Oxford, 1975).

Beaglehole, T.H., Thomas Munro and the Development of Administrative Policy in Madras, 1792-1818, The Origin of 'The Munro System' (Cambridge University Press, 1966).

Bearce, George D., British Attitudes Towards India 1784-1858 (Oxford University Press, 1961).

Beteille, Andre, Studies in Agrarian Social Structure (Delhi: OUP, 1974).

Briggs, A., The Age of improvement, 1783-1867 (London Longman, 1978).

Briggs, Henry George, The Nizam, His History and Relations with the British, 2 Vols. (London, 1861).

Ca Bishop Robert, A, Political and General History of the District of Tinnevelly In the Presidency of Madras From the Earliest Period to Its Cession to the English Government in A,D. 1801 (Madras, 1881).

Carpenter, Mary, Last Days of Raja Ram Mohun Roy in England (Calcutta, 1915).

Carrington, C.E., The British Overseas. Exploits of a Nation of Shopkeepers: Part I (Making' of the Empire), (Cambridge at the University Press, end edn. 1968).

Chand, Tarn, History of the Freedom Movement in India, Vol. 1 (Delhi: Publication Division, 1961).

Chandra, Bipan, The Rise and Growth of Economic Nationalism: Economic Policies of Indian National Leadership, 1880-1905 (New Delhi: PPH, 1982).

— ,Tripathi, Andes, and De, Barun, Freedom Struggle (New Delhi, 1980).

Chinnian P., The First Struggle for Freedom in India in 1806. Sporadic Events After the Vellore Mutiny (Erude, 1983).

Chitnis, K.N., Keladi Polizy (Dl KamatakiTmversity, 1974).

Chaudhuri, Shashi Bhusan, Civil Disturbances During the British Rule in India, 1765-1857 (Calcutta, 1

Das, Dipakranjan, Economic History of the Deccan From the First to the Sixth CenturyA.D. (Delhi, 1969).

Desai, A.R. (ed.), Peasant Struggles in India (Delhi, 1982).

Digby, William, India for Indians - and for England (London,1885).

Dua, J.C., Agrarian System in South India, Some Aspects (New Delhi, 1990).

_____,British Historiography: Eighteenth Century Punjab (New Delhi, 1992).

______,British In 'am Policy & Palegar Resistance in the Ceded Districts: Select Documents relating to Narasimha Reddy's Resistance 1846- 47(1994).

______,Palegars of South India: Forms and Contents of their Resistance in Ceded Districts (1996).

_______,Glossary of Revenue and Allied Terms of South India (1998),

_______,Illustrated Encyclopaedia & Who's Who of Princely States in Indian Sub-Continent (2000 & 2002).

______,Misl, Sikh State & The Institution of Khalsa (2006).

______,& Co. (ed.) Collected Works of Professor B.R. Grover of which two volumes namely — Land Rights, Landed Hierarchy & Village Community during Mughal Age and Medieval

Dutt, Romesh, The Economic History of India, Vol. I, Under Early British Rule (Delhi: Government of India, 1960).

Elliot, Sir Walter, Coins of Southern India (London, 1885).

Embree, Ainslie T. (ed.), India in 1857: The Revolt Against Foreign Rule (Delhi, 1987).

Fernandes, Praxy, Storm Over Seringapattam: The 1ncredib Story of Hyder All and Tipu Sultan (Bombay, 1969).

Flinn, M.W. (Selected and Ed.), Readings In Economic and Social History (London, 1st edn. 1964; Reprint 1945).

Frykenberg Robert Eric, Guntur District, 1788-1848; A History of Local Influence and Central Authority in South India (Oxford: Clarendon Press, 1965).

—, (ed.), Land Tenure and Peasant in South Asia (New Delhi, 1977; reprint, 1984).

—, (ed.), Land Control and Social Structure in Indian History (New Delhi, 1979).

Fraser, Cap. Hastings, Our Faithful Ally, The Nizam (London, 1865).

Gopal, M.H., The Finances of the Mysore State, 1799-1831 (Calcutta: Orient Longman, 1960).

—, Tipu Sultan 's Mysore: An Economic Study (Bombay, 1971).

Gopal, S., British Policy in India, 1858-1905 (Orient Longman, Indian edition, 1975).

Gough, Kathleen, Rural Society in South East India (London, 1981).

Gown, Mrs. K., Madurai Under the English East India Company 1801-1 857 (Madurai, 1987).

Gnbble, J.D. B., A History of the Deccan, 2 Vols. (London, 1924)

Guha, Nikhiles, Pre-British State System in South India: Mysore 1761-1799 (Calcutta, 1985).

Guha, Ranajit, A Rule of Property For Bengal: An Essay on the idea of Permanent Settlement (New Delhi: Orient Longman,1982).

Habib, Irfan, An Atlas of the Mughal Empire (OUP, 1986 print).

—, The Agrarian System of Mughal India (Asia Publishing House, 1963).

Hardgrave Jr., Robert L., The Nadars of Tamilnad: The Political Culture of a Community in Change (University of California Press, 1969).

Hasan, S. Nurul, Thoughts on Agrarian Relations in Mughal India (New Delhi, 1273, reprint 1983).

Hollingberry, William, .4 History of His Late Highness Nizam Alee K Soobah of the Deccan (Calcutta, 1805).

Iyengar, S. Sundaraja, Land Tenures in the Madras Presidency (Madras, 1933).

lyer, P.R. Ganapathi, The Law Relating to Hindu and Mohomedan Religious Endowments (Madras, 1905).

Judd, G.P., Members of Parliament 1734-1832 (New Haven, 1955).

Karashima, Noborn, South Indian History and Society; Studies From inscriptions, A.D. 850-1800 (Delhi: OUP, 1984).

Kareem, C.K., Kerala Under Haider All and Tipu Sultan (Co chin, 1973).

Khan, A.R., Chieftains in the Mughal Empire During the Reign of Akbar (Simla, 1977).

Khan, Mohibul Hasan, History of Tipu Sultan (Calcutta, 1951).

Krishnaswazni, P.R., Tom Munro Saheb Governor of Madras: Portrait with a Selection of his Letters (Madras, 1947).

Krishnaswami, S.Y., Rural Problems in Madras, Monograph (Madras, 1947).

Kumar, Dharma, Land and Caste in South India (London, 1965).

Kumar, Dharma, and Raychaudhuri, Tapan (Gen. Editors), The Cambridge Economic History of India, Vol. I C. 1200-C. 1750, (ed.), Tapan Raychaudhun and Irfan Habib; Vol. 11 C. 1757-C. 1970 (ed.), Dharma Kumar (Orient Longman in as sociation with Cambridge University Press, 1984).

Kuppuswamy, G.R., Economic Conditions in Karnataka (A.D. 973- A.D. 1336 (Dharwar: Karnatak University, 1975).

Lindsey, A.W.C., Life of Lindseys (Bangalore, 1849).

Ludden, David, Peasant History in South India (OUP, 1989).

Mahalingani, T.V., Administration and Social Life Unde. Vyayanagar, Part, I - Administration, Part II - Social L 2nd edn. (University of Madras, I, 1969; II, 1975).

______,South Indian Polity (Madras: Madras University, 1967).

Malcolm, Sir John, The Political History of India From 1784 to 1823, 2 V Vois. (London, 1826).

Marx, K., and Engels, F., The First Indian War of Independence 185 7-1859 (Moscow, undated. year of Russian Edn. 1959).

Metcalf, Thomas R., Land, Landlords, and the British Raj: Northern India in the Nineteenth Century (Delhi: OUP, 1979).

Misra, B.B., The Administrative History of India, 1834-194 7, General Administration (OUP, 1970).

Moore Jr., Barrington, Social Origins of Dictatorship: Lord and Peasant in the Making of the Modern World (Penguin Books, 1969).

Mukheijee, Nilmani, The Ryotwari System in Madras, '1792-1827 (Calcutta, 1962).

Nagaswamy, R. (ed.). South Indian Studies II (Society for Archaeological, Historical and Epigraphical Research, Madras, 1979).

Om Prakash, Early Indian Land Grants and Stale Economy (Allahabad, 1988).

Panigrahi, D.N., Charles Metcalfe in India: ideas and Administration 1806-1835 (New Delhi, 1968).

Philips, C.H., The East India Company 1784-1834 (Bombay: OUP, 1961).

Phillips, H.A.D., Our Administration of India (London, 1886).

Raghavaiyanger, S. Srinavasa, Memorandum of the Progress of the Madras Presidency During the Last Forty Years of British Administration (Madras: Government Press, 1893).

Raj, Jagdish, The Mutiny and British Land Policy in India (Bombay, 1965).

Rajayyan, K., Society and Administration in the Carnatic (Tirupathi, 1966).

— South Indian Rebellion: The First War of Independence 1800-1801 (Mysore, 1971).

— , Rise and Fall of the Poligars of Tamil Nadu (Madras, 1974).

— , History of Madurai 1736-1801 (Madurai University, Historical Series, Madurai, 1974).

R A. Sarda, Economic Conditions in the Madras Presidency, 1800-1850 (University of Madras, 1941).

Ramanappa, M.N. Venkata, Outlines of South Indian History (New Delhi, 1979)..

Ramesh K.V., A History of South Kanara (From the Earliest Times to the Fall of Vyayanagar), (Dharwar: Karnatak University, 1970).

Rao, A.V. Rainan, Economic Development of Andhra Pradesh 1766-1957 (Bombay, 1958).

Rao, C.V. Ramachandra, Administration and Society in Medieval Andhra Under the Later Eastern Ganges and Gajapatis (A.D. 1038 to 1538), (Nellore, 1976).

Rao, M. Ramachandra, The Development of Indian Polity (Madras, 1917).

Rao, P. Raghunadha, History of Modern Andhra (New Delhi, 1984).

Rainam, it, Agricultural Development in Madras State Prior to 1900 (Masras, 1966).

Raychaudhuri, Tapan, Jan Company in Coromandal: 1605-1690. Verhandelingen Van het Koninklijk Instituut Voor Taal-en Volkenkunde, Vol. XXXVIII (The Hague, 1962).

Reddy, Nagolu Krishna, Social History of Andhra Pradesh (Seventh to Thirteenth Century: Based on inscriptions and Literature), (Delhi, 1991).

Regani, Sarojini, Nizam-British Relations 1724-1857 (Hyderabad, 1963; New Delhi, 1988).

Richards, J.F., Mughal Administration in Golconda (Oxford,1975).

Roberts, P. E., India Under Wellesley (Gorakhpur, 1961).

Rothermund, Dietmar, The Indian Economy Under British Rule and Other Essays (New Delhi, 1983).

Roy, Raja Raminohan, Exposition of the Practical Operation of the Judicial and Revenue Systems of India (London, 1832).

Saran, P., Studies in Medieval Indian History (Delhi, 1952).

Sarkar, Jadunath, History of Aurangzeb, 5 Vols. (Calcutta, 1912-30), Vol. IV.

Sarma, P. Sree Rama, Saluva Dynasty of Vijayanagar (Hyderabad, 1979).

Sastri, K.A. Nilkanta, A History of South India From Pre- Historic Times to the Fall of Vyayanagar, 4th edn. (OUP, 1987)

____Sources of Indian History with Special Reference to South India (New York: Asia Publishing House, 1964).

____, The Colas, 2nd edn. (Madras: University of Madras, 1955).

____, and Srinivasachari, G., India: A Historical Survey (Allied Publishers, 1966).

Satyanarayana, K., A Study of the History and Culture of me Andhras: Volume One: From Stone Age to Feudalism (New Delhi: PPH, 1975).

Scott, David, Correspondence, 2 Vols. (London, 1951).

Seshan, K.S.S., British Role in Rural Economy (A Case Study of Punganur Zamindari), (New Delhi, 1989).

Shanmugain, P., The Revenue System of the Cholas, 850-1279 (Madras, 1987).

Shanna, M.H. Rama, The History of the V Empire, Vol. I, Beginning and Expansion, Vol. II, Decline and Disappearance, ed. by M.H. Gopal (Bombay, I, 1978; II, 1980).

Sharma, R.S., Survey of Research in Economic and Social History of India (Delhi, 1986).

Shore, Frederick John, Notes on Indian Affairs, Vol. I (London, undated, Date of 'Introduction', March 1836).

Shyam, Radhey, The Kingdom of Ahmednagar (Delhi, 1966).

Sircar, D.C. Studies in the Political and Administrative Systems in Ancient and Medieval India (Delhi, 1974).

— , Landlordism and Tenancy in Ancient and Medieval India as Revealed by Epigraphical Records (Lucknow: University of Lucknow 1969

Slater, Gilbert (ed.), Economic Studies, Vol. I, Some South Indian Villages (OUP, 1918).

Stem, Burton, Peasant State and Society in Medieval South/India (New Delhi: OUP, 1980).

Thomas Munro: The Origins of the Colonial State and His Vision of Empire (OUP, 1989).

Stokes, Eric, The English Utilitarians and India (Oxford, 1969).

____ The Peasant and the Raj: Studies in Agrarian Society and Peasant Rebellion in Central India (New Delhi, 1978).

Subrahmanian, N., Tamilian Historiography (Madurai, 1988).

Sutherland, L.S., The East India Company in Eighteenth Century Politics (Oxford Clarendon Press, 1952)

Temple, Sir Richard, Lord Lawrence (Macmillan, 1936).

Thurston, Edgar, Castes and Tribes of Southern India, 7 Vols. (Madras: Government Press, 1909), Vol. VII.

Veluthat Kesavan The Political Structure of Early Medieval South India (Orient Longman 1993).

Venkataramani, K.S., The Indian Village: A Ten Year Plan (Svetaranya Ashrama, Mylapore, Madrs, 1936).

Venkatasubramarian, T.K., Political Change and Agrarian Tradition in South India (C. 1600-1801), A Case Study (Delhi,.1986).

Verma, D.C., History of Bijapur (New Delhi, 1974).

Walter, Hamilton, A Geographical, Statistical and Historical Description of Hindustan and the Adjacent Countries, 2 Vols. (London, 1820; reprint, Madras, 1990).

14. Articles

Ali, M: Athar, 'The Eighteenth Century - An Interpretation', in Indian Historical Review, Vol. V. Nos, 1-2 (I.C.H.R.,-New Delhi, July 1978-January 1979).

Buckler, F.W., The Political Theory of the Indian Mutiny, Transactions of the Royal Historical Society, Fourth Series, Vol. V, 1922. Selections reproduced in Embree, Ainslie T., India, In 1857: The Revolt Against Foreign Rule (Delhi, 1987), pp. 95-103.

Dirks, N.B., 'Terminology and Taxonomy; Discourse and Domination: From Old Regime to Colonial Regime in South India', in Studies of South India. Eds. Robert Eric Frykenberg and Pauline Kolenda (Madras: New Era Publications, 1985).

Dua, J.C., 'Comparative Position of the Village Headmen During the Early British Rule in the Punjab and the Madras Presidency', Punjab History Conference, Patiala, 23rd session, 1987.

—, 'Landed Elites in Upheaval-Forms and Contents, of Resistance by the Palegars 1800-1846', Dr. Kalaignar Thiru M.Karunanidhi Endowment Lectures, Madras University, Madras, 7th, 10th, 11th April 1995.

____, 'Method of Land Measurement and Assessment in Northern Circars During the Pre-British Era as Reflected in the Chetri Ganitam', Indian History Congress, Dharwad, 1988.

_____, 'Nature of the Poligar Revolts in the Ceded Districts During the first Half of the 19th Century: A Case Study', Indian History Congress, Jadavpur, 1974....

____,'Review Article', on South Indian Rebellion: The First War of Independence, 1800-1801 by K. Raiayyan in The Indian Historical Review, Vol. II, No. 2, January 1976.

____, 'Poligars: Their Rise in the Ceded Districts', in Proceedings of Indian History Congress, 33rd session, 1972.

____, 'Position of the Patels and Karnams in the Ceded Districts during the 'First Quarter of the Nineteenth Century', Indian History Congress, Chandigarh, 1973. Also in Bhattacharya, Sabyasachi (ed.), Essays in Modern Indian Economic History (New Delhi, 1987).

Frykenberg, Robert Eric, 'The Silent Settlement in South India, 1793-1853: An Analysis of the Role of Inams in the Rise of the Indian ImperialSystem', in Frykenberg, Robert Eric (ed.), Land Tenure and Peasant in South Aisa (new Delhi, 1984).

'Traditional Process of Power and Administration in South India: An Historical Analysis of Local Influence', in Indian Economic and Social History Review, 1:2 (1963).

Ghosh, Benoy, 'Pre-Political Rebellions in Bengal', Frontier, Calcutta, Vol. V. Nos. 27-29, 14 October 1972.

Gough, Kathleen, 'Indian Peasant Uprisings', Economic and Political Weekly, Vol. IX, Non. 32-34, Special Number, August 1974.

Grover, B.R, 'An Analysis of the Contemporary Revenue Documents and Correspondence Pertaining to Patiala Chieftainship (Zamindari) during the later half of the 18th Century', Punjab past and present, Vol. XX1V-I, April 1990.

___ 'Nature of Land Rights in Mughal India', The Indian Economic and Social History Review, Vol. I, No. 1, 1963.

'Nature of Dehat-i-Taaluqa (Zamindari Villages) and the Evolution of the Taaluqdari System during Mughal Age', The Indian Economic and Social History Review, Vol. II. No 2, 1965 and Vol. II, No. 3, 1965.

___ 'Elements of Continuity and Change in the Land Ownership and Rights From the Mughal Age to the Early British Administration In India', Presidential Address, Medieval Indian Section, Indian History Congress, 37th Session, Calicut, 1976.

'The position of Desai in the Pargana Administration of Subah Gujrat under the Mughals', Indian History Congress, Delhi, 1961.

Hasan, S. Nural, 'The Position of the Zanundars in the Mughal Empire', The Indian Economic and Social History Review, Vol.

IV, 1964, also in Frykenberg, Robert Eric (ed.), Land Control and Social Structure in Indian History (New Delhi, 1979) under—the-title 'Zamindars Under the Mugbal'.

_____,'Three Studies of the Zamindari Systems, Medieval In dia: A Miscellany (Bombay, 1968).

_____,' Aspects of Zamindari System in Deccan', Indian History Congress, Varanasi 1969.

Hobsbawm, E 'Social Bandits: Reply (to Blok), in Comparative Studies in Society and History, Vol. XIV, No. 4, September 1972.

Jagannadham, A., 'Some Aspects of Socio-Economic Conditions in Ceded -Districts: 1800-1810', Itihas (Hyderabad), Vol. IV, No. 2 19-76.

Komarov, Erik 'Content and Principal Forms of the Evolution of Agrarian Relations in India in the 19th Century', New India Studies by Soviet Scholars, - "Social 5'ciences To day", No. 33, 1976.

Krishna, M.R., The Dalvai Family of Mysore', in Bharat Kaumudi, Studies In Indo logy In Honour of Dr. Radha Kumud Mookerji, Part I (Allahabad, 1945).

Moreland, W.H., 'Feudalism(?) in the Moslem Kingdom of Delhi', Journal of Indian 'History, Vol. VII, Part I, 1938.

Murthy, M.L.K., 'Environment, Royal Policy and Social Formation in the Eastern South India, A.D., 1000-1500,' Presidential Address, Historical Archaeology, Epigraphy and Numismatic Section, Indian History Congress, 53 rd session, Warangal, 1992-93.

Murton, B., 'Key People in the Countryside: Decision -making in Interior Tamilnadu in the Late Eighteenth Century Country side', The Indian Social and Economic History Review, Vol. II No. 2, June 1973.

Narayana, Dr. D.L., Professor of Economics, S.V. University,. Tirupathi, 'Famines in Rayalaseema', An unpublished article in Tamil Nadu State Archives, Madras.

Ran, B.S.L. Hanumantha, 'The Boyas in Andhra History; Journal of Andhra Historical Research Society, 38, 1983-84, pp. 77

Rao, Diwan BahaLlur T. Bhujanga, 'Rayalaseema;, in Journal of the Andhra Historical Research Society, Vol. XVII, Part 1-4, July-October 1946 - January-April 1947.

Rao, R. Subba, 'A Brief Account of the Political Organisation and Economic -Conditions, Religion and Literature of Andhradesa Between 225-6 10 A.D.', Indian History Congress, 1953.

Rau, D.S. Achute, 'Haider Mi, His Relations with the Crown', Indian Historical Records Commission Proceedings, XVIII Meeting, Mysore, January 1942.

Reddy, M. Pattabhi Rama, 'Aspects of Agrarian Revolution in Andhra (1800-1820): The Munro System.- Extermination of Poligars;, Proceedings of Andhra Pradesh History Congress, Ramachandrapuram, 1976.

Richards, JF., 'The Hyderabad Karnatik, 1687-1707', in Modern Asian Studies, Vol. IX, 1975.

Sen, Asok, 'A Pre-British Economic Formation in India of the Late Eighteenth century', in Barun De (ed.), Perspectives in Social Sciences (I): Historical Dimensions (Calcutta, 1977).

Seshan, K.S.S., 'Chittoor Palegarla Viplavam' (Telegu), in K. Veerabhadra Rao (ed.), Telugu (A Quarterly devoted to Sci ence and Humanities), Vol. VI, No. 2 (Telugu Akademi, Hyderabad, 1979).

Sherwani, H.K., 'The Reign of Abdu'l Qutb Shah (1626-1672):

Economic Aspects -I', Journal of Indian History, XLII (Au gust 1964), II, XLV (December 1967).

Sinha, J.C., 'Economic Conditions of the Ceded Districts (1800-1807', Indian Historical Records Commission, Proceedings of Vol. XVII, December 1940.

Shinivasachari, C.S., 'The Polegar System - Its Development and Decay', Journal ofMadras University, Vol. III, 1955.

___ 'The Poligar System in the Tamil Country : Its Origin and Growth', in Indian Historical Records Commission Proceedings, XI, 1928.

Stein, Burton, 'Idiom and Ideology in Early Nineteenth Century South India', in Peter Robb (ed.), Rural India: Land Power and Society Under British Rule (London Curzon Press, 1983).